CORPORATE RECRUITER TELLS ALL

Tips, Secrets, and Strategies
From a Corporate Recruiter

Ryan Fisher

ISBN: 1469933187
ISBN 13: 9781469933184

Library of Congress Control Number: 2012901323
CreateSpace, North Charleston, SC

TABLE OF CONTENTS

INTRODUCTION

It pains me to see so many people working day after day at unsatisfying jobs with limited opportunities and unrewarding compensation. Better jobs and higher salaries are within the grasp of many of these people. Yet, they are unable to obtain them because they don't know how. Are you in this predicament? If so, you've picked up the right book.

In these pages, I'll tell you how to get the job of your dreams with the financial returns you deserve. You'll learn about the most common mistakes made by job candidates, so you can avoid them. I'll give you inside tips that most other job seekers don't know and most recruiters won't divulge. I'll show you how recruiters and hiring managers truly think. I'll deliver this information with brutal honesty, without glossing over harsh realities or indulging in political correctness.

My goal is to help you land a position where you can use your unique skills and earn what you're worth. Who doesn't want to earn more money with their talents? I don't want you to be shortchanged in your career or in your life.

Over my twelve-plus years as a professional recruiter, I've witnessed some unfortunate mistakes:

- I've seen job candidates accept as much as $15,000 less per year in salary or more than they could have obtained because they didn't know how to negotiate.

- I've seen great candidates fail to get interviews because their resumes did not demonstrate the level of expertise that they possessed.

- I've seen highly qualified candidates fail to get jobs because they lacked interviewing skills.

- And I've seen extremely competent candidates become discouraged because they didn't understand how the system works.

This book is based on my experiences as a recruiter in a variety of settings, including a recruiting agency, a small business, and a publicly held company with more than $1 billion dollars in annual sales. In a typical year, it was not unusual for me to

- Review more than 20,000 resumes

- Speak to thousands of job seekers

- Arrange hundreds of interviews

- Negotiate hundreds of offers

I learned many strategies and secrets during those years, and I'll share them all with you. You'll learn what works and what to watch out for, so you can gain the inside track to the job of your choice.

I'll tell you

- How one of my clients got offers for $23,000 dollars above her current salary.

- How a single sentence empowered one job candidate to negotiate for an additional $15,000 dollars per year in salary on top of what he had already negotiated within three minutes.

- How another client negotiated a $40,000 dollar increase in his base salary, even though the hiring manager didn't want to pay it.

- How I personally negotiated an increase in my base annual salary from $50,000 dollars to $100,000 dollars.

I'll also tell you about creative strategies for bypassing normal channels and getting your foot in the door, even if you aren't a perfect fit for the position. Not only did I use these techniques to land an interview for the job of my dreams that most people would assume I wouldn't be able to land, I engineered the whole thing from the opposite side of the country. You'll be able to do the same thing, after reading this book.

This book will give you the inside scoop that you need in order to understand and conquer the job market. For example,

- Did you ever apply for a job for which you were a perfect fit, only to never hear back? I'll tell why that might have happened and what you can do to avoid it.

- Did you know that companies may fill up to 50 percent of their job openings through employee referrals? I'll show you how to network your way to your next career!

- Are you aware of the two key factors that motivate recruiters? I'll tell you what they are and how you can use them to influence recruiters to work hard for you!

- Did you know that some people are surreptitiously eliminated from consideration for a job opening based on rumors before they even get to the interview? I'll tell you why this happens and how you can keep it from happening to you.

But that's not all. In this book, I also cover such key topics as

1. How to clarify where you are now and what you want in the future

2. How to create a job search plan

3. How to figure out what you are worth

4. How to write a winning resume that gets you the interview

5. How to prepare for interviews, so you will impress the hell out of any hiring manager

6. How to follow up after the interview to increase your chances on getting an offer

7. How to negotiate the best offer possible!

The goal of this book is to help you find and secure the job that will enable you to realize your full potential. If that's what you want, then let's get started!

Chapter 1

UNDERSTAND THE HIRING PROCESS

Have you ever wondered why some job candidates are passed over (perhaps you've been one of them), even though their skills, experience, personality, and salary requirements are a perfect fit for a position? To understand this phenomenon, you need to understand the dynamics of the hiring process. Perhaps, the best way to illustrate the dynamics of the hiring process is though a hypothetical scenario.

The Case of the Pressured Sales Manager

Imagine that you are a sales manager for Microsoft, and you have five direct reports. Further assume that each salesperson is responsible for bringing in sales of $100,000 dollars per month or $1.2 million per year. This means that you are personally responsible for an annual sales quota of $6 million dollars.

Now, let's further suppose that one of your direct reports resigns. Does that reduce your quota? Of course it doesn't. You are still responsible for bringing in $6 million dollars of sales a year. Since the salesperson who left had been producing about $100,000 dollars of revenues per month, you're probably going to fall that much short of your quota every month while this position is vacant.

Obviously, you're under a lot of pressure to fill the position! If it takes you about a month and a half to hire a replacement (and it can take longer than that) and the new hire needs to give two week's notice to his current employer, then you've already lost two months of revenues, which in our example amounts to $200,000 dollars. What's more, this new person will need to be trained, so it might take a while before his sales get up to the average of $100,000 dollars per month.

And what if the new hire doesn't perform as well as you had hoped? Maybe his sales are merely $50,000 dollars per month for the first five months, instead of $100,000 dollars per month. After five months, you'll be an additional $250,000 dollars short of your quota, bringing your total deficit to $450,000 dollars. You'll probably miss your quota for the year, which means you might lose a portion of your commission and perhaps your entire bonus.

But it could get even worse. If the new hire doesn't work out after several months on the job, then you'll need to start the hiring process all over again. Meanwhile, as you continue to miss quotas, your boss will start to take notice of your lack of performance. And if things don't turn around, your job could be in jeopardy.

And that's still not all, at least from the standpoint of the company. Employee turnover is expensive, and these lost revenues are only part of the overall cost. You also need to consider the cost of finding, hiring, and training the new hire. What if this new salesperson creates some problems that need to be fixed? How much will that cost you? How much time and effort will you have to put forth into firing that underperformer?

The Essence of Hiring

Against the background provided by the previous scenario, can you now more readily recognize the major dynamic at play in the hiring process? When you dig down deep and look at this process at a fundamental level, what is the essence of hiring?

I maintain that in essence hiring is *risk management.* That is to say, the primary motivation of hiring managers and their companies is to avoid mistakes that will cost the company and hiring manager time, stress, and money.

You might not like this answer. In fact, this play-it-safe approach might not be the best one for the company that's doing the hiring. Yet, more often than not, it's how companies behave. Simply put, hiring managers don't like to take risks.

So, how does this affect you as a job candidate? It means that if you want to get hired, you must do everything possible to convince the hiring manager and others involved in the hiring process that you are a safe bet. While it's *good* to be seen as the candidate who has the most upside potential, it's *vital* to be viewed as the candidate who is least likely to fail.

Branding

How do you present this image? The answer is that you must build trust through branding. Your brand is derived from your personal referrals and references and through your associations with people and organizations (the schools you attended, the businesses you worked for, and so forth).

To illustrate the concept of branding, suppose a manager at Facebook is looking for a software engineer. Which of these two resumes do you think will rise to the top of the pile?

- Candidate A, who has five years of experience at Google
- Candidate B, who has ten years of similar experience at a company with little or no name recognition.

Because recruiters and hiring managers spend on average of only 15 to 30 seconds glancing over a resume, the word Google is going to immediately pull most of them toward candidate A. The former Google employee may have not done a good job there, but that bit of information is almost secondary. The hiring manager knows who Google is, and the business model and culture of Google is probably closer to Facebook's. So, candidate A will be perceived as less risky.

If the manager hires candidate B and this decision doesn't work out, his boss may start asking a lot of questions: Where did you find this person? What company did he work for? Did you ask the right questions during the interview? Did you check references?

On the other hand, if he hires candidate A and that decision doesn't work out, he can always say to his boss, "We hired him from Google. He was there for five years, and he passed our interviews, so we thought he would be okay." That is probably going to be an acceptable answer. Perhaps, now you understand why most hiring managers consciously or unconsciously favor candidates who have worked for their direct competitors or with companies with similar business models.

No one likes to be scrutinized and criticized over bad hiring decisions. Bad hiring decisions are glaringly apparent, while mediocre hiring decisions are barely noticed. It's no wonder that most managers choose the safe route.

I used a sales manager example because it made the risks easy to quantify. However, all management jobs present similar risks. Here are some other examples:

- If you're a help desk manager and you hire someone who is unable to adequately answer technical questions, how will that affect the level of service your group provides? How much will this deficiency cost your company? What will it cost you personally?

- As a payroll supervisor, if you hire someone who is careless and messes up employees' paychecks, how long will that situation be tolerated? And if the problem mushrooms, how long will you be tolerated?

- Suppose you are a project manager, and you add someone to your team who can't do the job. If your project falls behind schedule, what do you think the reaction will be as the poor performance of your project impacts other areas of the business?

When things go bad, you as the supervisor are responsible. Shifting blame to your direct reports seldom works. This is why it is so much easier for hiring managers to play it safe throughout the hiring process and say no to candidates who present the slightest risk.

A Real-Life Branding Illustration

While working for a recruiting agency, I was seeking to fill a high-level software sales position. The base salary was $100,000 dollars, with the potential for another $100,000 dollars in commissions.

When I asked the hiring manager what he was looking for in a candidate, he said that the ideal hire will have worked in software sales with a company similar to his, and he went on to list several specific companies that qualified. Then, he said he would also consider candidates who went to any Ivy League school, even if they had no sales experience. I asked the manager why he attached such importance to certain schools. He said, "If they were good enough to get into one of those schools, we know we can train them to do the job."

You and I know that going to Harvard or Princeton or Yale or some other prestigious school doesn't guarantee success, especially in sales. However, some schools have such strong brands that they inherently project a strong degree of trust. That was certainly true for this particular hiring manager.

Hiring managers give recruiters this kind of guidance all the time. We're told that candidates must have attended certain schools, attained a certain level of education, and worked for certain companies. None of these factors guarantee success. In fact, they're probably not even the most important ingredients for success. However, hiring managers stress them because of the branding effect. They don't want to take chances.

If at any point in the hiring process you do anything that raises a question about your ability to do the job, then you probably won't get the job. The hiring manager will find it easier to say no than to take the risk, especially if she has been burned by a bad hire in the past. If you were the hiring manager, you'd probably seek to protect yourself in the same way.

The good news is that there are plenty of methods for getting around a hiring manager's aversion to risk, and the even better news is that most job candidates aren't using any of these methods. So, if you employ them, you will truly stand out from the crowd. I will go over these techniques in the succeeding chapters.

Chapter 2

BE PROACTIVE

If you want to pursue the career of your dreams and obtain the compensation you desire, you need to be proactive about your job search. You must determine where you want to go and how you will get there. Then, you must take the necessary actions to achieve your goals.

No one is going to live your life for you. You must take charge and make things happen. Jobs won't just come to you. You must find them.

Did you know that some job openings are never advertised? For many jobs that are advertised, you might not have a chance of being considered because the hiring manager already knows who he is going to hire. If you don't find out about job openings through research and networking, and if you don't let others (including your boss) know about your goals, how can you expect to be considered for these positions?

Why You Should Be Proactive

One of my clients routinely gave me a few positions to work on every month. During the two years I worked with this company, I never saw one of those openings posted on their career website. I don't know if this was deliberate or an oversight. Regardless, these jobs could only be uncovered through networking or by the slim chance that a recruiter or someone else stumbled across a candidate's resume.

Every company has job openings that for various reasons aren't advertised. Some are kept confidential because the company plans to terminate the person currently holding the position. Many times, positions aren't advertised because hiring managers already know who they want to hire. I have seen companies take this approach for all levels of positions, from entry-level employees all the way up to executive vice presidents. If you haven't cultivated relationships, you won't even be considered for these positions.

Proactive job seekers look for career advancement opportunities *before* they need them. Their eyes and ears are always open. They're constantly talking to people to learn more about the job market, and they have their ideal career path clearly in mind. Consequently, if they do decide to make a move, they will have a head start and can proceed with thoughtful intentionality.

Reactive job seekers don't think about their career moves until circumstances force them to. Then, they get desperate. Often, they make unwise decisions based on insufficient information. They settle for less pay and satisfaction than they could have achieved with more time and planning.

If you take your time and find the job of your dreams, just imagine how much happier you will be than if you rushed the process and compromised. I understand that sometimes you may need to find a job *now*. Still, being proactive will still help you conduct a better job search. Proactive job seekers are able to choose the *best* opportunities. They don't have to settle for "good enough."

Tip

A senior-level executive once gave me the best job search advice I ever received. He said, "Give yourself six months to find a new job. Make sure you have two offers in hand, and then decide which one you prefer."

"Have your friends before you need them," said Bob Johnson, the billionaire founder of Black Entertainment Television. He's right. If your networking relationships are already in place and your knowledge of the competitive job market is current, you are much more likely to land the job of your dreams.

To get ahead, sometimes you need to target the job you want and the company you want to work for. After you find them, sell them on you. This takes time and focused effort.

At one time, I found a job I really wanted and, in an upcoming chapter, I'll tell you how I landed that interview. However, at this point, I simply want to mention that when I first approached the company, it took them more than two months to respond. At that time, they didn't have an opening that fit my interests and qualifications, but a few months later they did. If I had been passive instead of proactive, they never would have considered me.

The Job Pyramid

The job market can be thought of as a pyramid. As you move up the career ladder, the number of available opportunities decreases. For example, in any company, numerous people work in lower-level positions, fewer people work in managerial positions, and only one person is the CEO. Within a software development department, there will be many software engineers and far fewer *lead* software engineers. Generally speaking, the higher up you go, the more time will be required to find a new position that meets your criteria.

Let's say you are a software engineer making $120,000 dollars per year. When you first enter the job market, you might be unable to find any opportunities that pay more than $115,000 dollars. If you need to find a job immediately, then you might be forced to make a lateral move to even accept a pay cut. I often see people settle for $10,000 dollars less in annual pay than they could have obtained because they were in a rush and didn't have time to thoroughly search the market.

Making a lateral move or taking a pay cut is not necessarily bad. People do it all the time, and it might be the best route to where you ultimately want to go. However, for most people, it's an act of desperation. If they had cultivated a larger network, then they probably could have found a better opportunity that provided them with a higher level of compensation or other advantages that they were looking for in a new job.

Risks of Not Being Proactive

Recently, I worked with a candidate who had been laid off from a job paying $85,000 dollars per year. I referred him to a position with a target salary of $75,000 dollars and a maximum salary of $85,000 dollars. During the interview, he said he hoped his new salary would at least match his previous one, but the hiring manager held firm, so the candidate accepted the offer.

This candidate had absolutely no bargaining leverage. Not only was he unemployed, he had no other job offers. If he had insisted on more money, the hiring manager might have called his bluff and given the job to someone else.

If this candidate had been working an established network, he might have had other interviews and offers in his pocket. This would have empowered him to hold out for more money or hold off accepting the job until he could interview with more companies. I see this scenario with a lot of job candidates. Because they do not proactively cultivate multiple options in advance, they are left with little or no negotiating leverage when they need it.

Throughout this book, you will learn how to discover what you are worth, how to build a network, and how to leverage these assets to secure the best job possible. I'll cite actual examples of candidates who successfully negotiated for higher compensation as well as examples of candidates who were unable to obtain their objectives, so you can learn from their experiences.

Salary Isn't Everything

Landing a job with a good salary is important, but it's even more important to find a position that allows you to realize your full potential. You'll be more likely to find such a position if you proactively take the time in advance to clarify what you want and develop a strategy to go after it.

If you're in sales, you can become a sales manager or vice president of sales if that's what you want. It happens! If you're a software engineer, you can move up to engineering manager or vice president of engineering. If you are unable to get the growth opportunity you desire at your current company, you can make it happen outside your company. You can do it, if you're proactive!

Chapter 3

KNOW WHAT YOU WANT

Before you can begin any journey, you need to know where you are and where you're going. Similarly, before you begin your job search, you need to be clear about your current situation and your goals. You can't find the job of your dreams if you don't know what your dreams are. You need to know what you really want in a job, in a company, in a compensation level, and in a responsibility level.

If you don't know what you're aiming for, you could end up wasting a lot of time moving about and going nowhere. Too many people make one lateral move after another. They don't stay long in any one job because of lack of clarity, which causes them to keep taking jobs that offer limited satisfaction and growth potential. If these job seekers focused their time and energy on finding the right situation, they wouldn't need to move on so quickly. Such positions do exist, but they usually don't come knocking on your door. You have to seek them out, and you can't seek them out if you don't know what you want.

The Benefits of Knowing What You Want

Someone I am currently coaching is taking her time interviewing with different companies. Because she knows what she wants and what the top people in her field earn, she is getting offers of $23,000 dollars more than her current base salary. And because she is presently working at home about half the time, all the companies she is talking to have been offering her the same working arrangement.

For the first two months of her job search, not one company offered her this amount of salary increase or the ability to work part time at home. Yet, now that she is clear about what she wants, she conveys these expectations up front in every interview, and now virtually every company has been willing to meet them. If they aren't willing to meet her expectations, then she moves on from that opportunity right away.

Another interesting thing has happened during this woman's job search. She has realized that money is not the most important factor. Her current job offers lots of flexibility, which is really important to her. Because she has two small children, the ability to come in late or leave early is a big plus. She also appreciates the confidence her superiors place in her by allowing her to work rather independently. No one attempts to micromanage her.

As she has progressed through her job search, she's come to the conclusion that her present job offers her benefits that would be hard to match. In particular, her flexible schedule allows her to very satisfactorily balance her personal and professional goals. More money would be nice, but she's realizing that flexibility and independence are nicer.

Therefore, she's decided to stay put for now. Yet, the time she spent searching for a job was not in vain. She has a huge network that she has created, which she can draw upon if she ever decides to make a change. When and if that time comes, she probably will be able to find a new job very quickly.

Gaining Clarity

Below are some assessments that will help you gain clarity about where you are now, what you are looking for, and where you want to ultimately be. Keep in mind that these assessments are just a start. Like the woman

I mentioned previously, you might only learn exactly what you want after you get out there and start talking to companies. However, answering the following questions should begin to give you additional clarity.

Self-Assessment

Part 1: Where are you now?

1. What is your current job?

2. What do you like about your current job and current company?

NOTE: This is really important. I have seen plenty of candidates go on interview after interview, only to eventually realize that an extra $10,000 or $15,000 dollars in salary is not as important as some of the benefits they enjoy in their current position.

3. What do you dislike about your current job and current company?

NOTE: Think long and hard about this. Consider whether the situation you presently dislike is temporary or permanent. If temporary, you may just need to be patient. If more permanent, then possibly you can do something to resolve the issue. For example, if you work for a large company, you might be able to request a move to a new department or to a different project.

4. Why are you looking for a new job?

5. What are your current salary and benefits?

NOTE: You need to keep your salary and benefits information in mind, in case you need to recall this information on a moment's notice. If a hiring manager starts to negotiate with you, you will need to know your starting point.

Part 2: Short Term Goals

1. What type of salary, benefits, and job title do you desire?

NOTE: When you begin your search, you should know exactly what you are looking for from a compensation standpoint. If you don't, you may settle for less than you can get.

2. What do you hope to gain by working in a new job for a new company?

3. What type of position are you looking for in another company?

4. Would you prefer to work for a startup, a fast-growing company, a large company, a nonprofit organization, or in some other environment?

   NOTE: Usually, startups and fast-growing companies offer more upside potential, while large companies might offer more security. Other factors, such as office politics and the amount of structure, can also be important.

5. What type of culture do you prefer? For example, are you looking for a young company that is working on cutting-edge technology, or would you like a more conservative environment?

Part 3: Long Term Goals (where do you want to be in five, ten, or fifteen years)?
1. What do you want to be doing?

2. What level of compensation do you want?

3. Is the job you are considering on the path to where you want to eventually be?

Note: Anyone can go out and get a job. However, if you want to be successful, then you must develop clear goals and align your actions with them.

Chapter 4

DO YOUR RESEARCH

Once you determine your career goals and before you start interviewing, do your research. Make a list of all the companies in your area you'd like to work for. Then, collect information about them and use that information to narrow your list.

Talk with people who used to work with these companies. If you don't know anyone directly, you probably know someone who knows someone who did. You can also check out employers using the internet. Glassdoor. com is a free site that gives you insider information about the salaries, benefits, and working conditions of various companies. TheVault.com is a similar site that charges a fee. Most of the information comes from current or previous employees, so you have to take it with a grain of salt. Some of them might have axes to grind, and any bad experiences they had may not apply to you.

On the flip side, a company that gets rave reviews may not be your best choice. Even at the greatest company in the world, your boss could turn out to be a jerk, or there might be other factors that would make an environment a poor fit for you. You won't know about some of these things until you interview.

After you narrow down your list to your top five companies, start conducting some in-depth research. Ask questions about each company, such as the following:

- Is this company growing?

- Will it provide me with career growth? (Every company says it will, but not all deliver on that promise. However, if the company is growing, there is a greater chance that you will have room to grow with it.)

- Does this company seem to have a culture where I will enjoy working?

- Is the company profitable?

Concerning this last question, it's rather easy to assess the financial condition of publicly held companies because their financial statements are readily available. However, what if a company is privately held? You can still glean quite a bit of information from its website and on the internet. Most companies like to brag about awards they have won, new business they have obtained, new products they have introduced, and other significant achievements.

Try to determine using LinkedIn how many people are leaving the company. Considerable turnover, especially within an executive team, probably isn't a good sign. Also check the job postings on the company's career website. If there are only a few, be cautious.

Not Doing Your Research Can Be Costly: A Real-Life Example

Now, I'm going to tell you how to avoid a common mistake that could not only cost you your job, but even your house! A large, publicly held company where I once worked hired a woman who was going to be a director of a group. Three days before she was supposed to start, after she had already given notice to her employer, the new company called her and rescinded its offer. The reason was lack of funding. By the way, this woman was six months pregnant.

Around the same time, this company also laid off some senior-level executives who had recently been hired. At first, I felt really bad for these people. This happened during a recession, and it was probably going to be hard for them to find new jobs. Then, I realized this unfortunate incident was 100 percent their fault. Why do I say that? I have already given you enough information to figure this out, but I'll tell you anyway.

All of these people were successful mangers, executives, and directors with lots of work experience. Some had been responsible for managing hundreds of people and overseeing millions and millions of dollars. If they had taken just a few minutes to do some basic online research, they would have seen that this publicly held company had been not just losing money for the last year and a half, but bleeding money. Furthermore, they could have discerned that its direct competitors where growing at rates ranging from 10 to 20 percent.

Why would they go to work for a company that was losing money, while its competitors were growing by leaps and bounds? These financial results should have been a huge red flag. I understand that if you are new to the job market or if you're desperate for a job, you may have to overlook these danger signals. However, these people were getting paid hundreds of thousands of dollars to be corporate leaders, and they should have done their homework. Ten minutes of research could have saved them an incredible amount of pain, heartache, and loss. I'm excusing the company, mind you. It was a bonehead move to make these job offers because the money and the business just weren't there. Yet, these people should have known better.

All these executives took their jobs based on the name brand of the company and the relationships they had in place. Those things are important, but at the end of the day, they will only get you so far. (Of course, if you work on Wall Street, these rules don't apply. The federal government will bail your company out, so you'll get your rewards anyway.)

By the way, if a company is losing money, even if you're not laid off, how big do you think your raise or bonus is going to be? What growth opportunities are going to exist for you in a company that is shrinking? When layoffs are occurring all around you, how stressed out are you going to be wondering if you're next? I can tell you from experience it's not a fun time when your conversations with co-workers focus on where the axe is going to fall and whether the company will survive. The culture totally changes when half the people you knew are gone and the halls that once buzzed with excitement fall silent.

Doing Your Research Can Help You: A Real-Life Example

At one time, I considered moving to the San Francisco Bay area, so I could work for a Silicon Valley company. However, I was living on the East Coast, and I didn't know a soul who had ever worked out there. One day, a previous co-worker happened to mention that she had a friend who used to work at Apple and some other high-tech companies in that area, and she offered to put me in touch with her.

A few weeks later, this friend of a friend and I had a long phone conversation. She told me about the companies she had worked for, which ones she liked best, and what I might be able to get for a salary. Most importantly, she volunteered to put me in touch with some of the hiring managers she knew. How cool was that? I didn't even have to ask for these referrals.

At the time, I wasn't ready to make the move. I just wanted to survey the employment landscape. Yet, I tell this story to emphasize the importance of talking to as many people as possible about your career goals. You never know what might develop.

It's so much better to know the important facts about a company in advance. Once you've quit your job and started work with a new employer, you're highly vulnerable. Some pretty unpleasant surprises can lurk behind closed doors. It doesn't take much research in person and online to determine which companies are brutal to work for. Why take a risk? Do your research, so you can expand your opportunities and minimize your unknowns.

Chapter 5

KNOW WHAT
YOU'RE WORTH

Knowing what you are worth and having an idea of what compensation you can get are two of the most important pieces of information you must have before you start salary negotiations. Without this information, you could ask for a $12,000 dollar salary increase, even though the company might be able to give you a $25,000 dollar increase. If you had all of this information, would you simply ask for a $12,000 dollar increase and leave the other $13,000 dollars on the table?

Don't laugh! That's what the vast majority of candidates do all the time. Maybe you've done it yourself. Have you ever wondered where that extra money goes? Perhaps, the CEO and the other executives will use it to pay their own salaries and bonuses. Those huge amounts have to come from somewhere. Apparently, they're asking for them and getting them, and so can you!

There's another reason you should know how much you're worth. If you ask for too much, you could price yourself out of a job. If you have an idea of what companies can pay and where you stand in relationship to the going rates, you will have a lot more power and confidence when it comes time to negotiate. In this chapter, I'll show you some valuable techniques to help you figure out what you are worth!

Be Aware of Wide Disparities in Salaries

You should be aware that most companies have considerable latitude with salaries. In fact, at many companies, people who work in the same groups and who do the same type of work may have great differences in pay. Of course, the companies will try to disguise this by giving employees different job codes and different internal titles, when outside the company these mean absolutely nothing. But internally this provides some rationalization for the disparities.

Real-Life Example

I once worked for a company where several recruiters were doing essentially the same kind and amount of work, but their annual salaries varied by as much as $45,000 dollars. Admittedly, some of them were "senior recruiters" who had five more years of experience than the junior recruiters, but the responsibilities and the productivity all were about equal. What's more, among the senior recruiters, some who were doing an incredible job were getting paid $20,000 dollars less than other senior recruiters with the same number of years of experience. I am willing to bet that if those recruiters who were getting paid less knew earlier what the salary ranges were, they would have asked for more money, and they could have gotten it.

Don't think for a minute that this only happens to recruiters. I regularly hire people at salaries that are $10,000, $15,000, or $20,000 dollars less than what the company is willing to pay or paying other people for the same work. And when it comes time to negotiate salaries with these candidates, I sit on the phone just praying that they will ask for more money because I know they can get it if they ask.

The Importance of Asking

You can't always get more money by asking, but you will never know until you do ask. I'll go over this in greater detail in the chapter on negotiating. In the meantime, the easiest way for you to get a higher salary and better compensation is to find out what people in your field are earning in your local area. Once you have this information, negotiating your salary will be a whole lot easier.

We can learn a lot from real estate brokers. Before they list a home, they research the market and find out what comparable housing units are selling for. Then, they price accordingly. Fortunately, modern technology allows you to easily do a bit of online research and apply the same approach when preparing for your salary negotiations.

I once had a client who got a $40,000 dollar raise over his last salary, simply because he knew what he was worth and that that was the going rate for candidates with his level of experience in his field. The hiring manager cringed at having to give him that much of an increase, but she knew that she was going to have to pay that amount to someone to fill the position. Keep in mind, however, that he only got it because he asked and did not back down from that request during the negotiation.

As I mentioned earlier, a woman I am currently coaching is fielding offers of $23,000 dollars more than her current salary because she knows what the top candidates get paid in her industry. I personally was able to increase my base salary by $50,000 dollars when I changed jobs because I found out what the average companies paid top recruiters.

It Pays to Know What You Are Worth: A Real-Life Example

When I was thinking about moving to the San Francisco Bay area, as I mentioned in the previous chapter, I checked Google's website and job boards, but I didn't see any listings for recruiters. So, I went to LinkedIn and found a lead contract recruiter at that company who had posted his e-mail address.

I sent this recruiter an e-mail, along with my resume. I didn't tell him I was actively seeking a job because I wasn't at that time. However, I did let him know that I was interested in moving to his area, and I asked him how much contract recruiters were getting paid. After looking over my resume, he replied via e-mail that I could probably bill out at around $70 to $80 dollars per hour.

In the region where I currently worked, contract recruiters typically bill out at $50 dollars per hour. If I had moved west and interviewed without doing my research, I probably would have asked for $25 or $30 dollars less per hour than the companies were willing to pay. In other words, I could have left $50,000 dollars per year on the table.

The information this recruiter provided was extremely helpful. He also invited me to connect with him on LinkedIn, and he offered to get me an interview at Google if I decided to move out his way. Notice how much help I got by spending fifteen minutes searching for recruiters at Google and five minutes e-mailing one!

Obviously, this approach for gathering information and making contacts would work for any part of the country. In fact, if you utilized these techniques a few minutes every day, you soon would have built up a powerful network for generating information and referrals. Such a network would come in mighty handy when you need to change jobs.

You also can find out what you're worth by asking people you know, but you have to be careful. There is always the possibility that the information you receive is inaccurate or out of date. I run into this problem two to three times a year.

A Real-Life Example

Not long ago, I was trying to fill a position that paid around $150,000 a year. When it came time to negotiate the salary, the candidate insisted on receiving $300,000 a year. That was ludicrous! Even the vice presidents in this company weren't making that much. But she had been told by a friend what she should be getting, and she wouldn't accept any other answer.

These people with unrealistic expectations tend to be very difficult to deal with. As we coach them about the facts, they come crashing down to earth faster than a satellite that's been knocked out of orbit. My point is to be sure to consult multiple sources as you seek to determine your worth. If possible, check with people who work for the company you are targeting for employment.

Two websites I mentioned in the last chapter, Glassdoor.com and TheVault.com, can provide useful salary information. There are a few other websites that also provide this information, but they aren't as reliable. And while those websites may provide a good starting point to figure out what you are worth, you will get a much better idea of your worth by talking to people who work in your field.

Interviewing to Learn What You Are Worth

After you have an idea of what you might be worth, the best way to refine your information is to start interviewing. Start with companies that are at the bottom of your list, so you can test the waters without fear of knocking yourself out of contention for a job you really want.

Tip

Never begin a conversation or a correspondence with the question, "How much does this job pay?" I'm so sick of this. If someone I'm considering for a position leads off with that question, I pull the plug. Of course, this question is legitimate after you have established mutual rapport.

It's usually easier to find out what a company pays after you have revealed the salary you desire. One approach is to answer a salary query with something like, "Well, I am a little bit flexible on salary. I would consider $115,000 for the right opportunity. Would that be within your range?"

Now that you have laid your cards on the table, a recruiter may consider it only fair to tell you what the company considers reasonable. Many recruiters may be straightforward with you because they don't want to waste their time. Recruiters at agencies will normally be upfront with you about what a position can pay because that is usually their standard practice. Also keep in mind that it's much easier to extract information from someone when you are speaking to each other in person or on the phone.

If there is a wide gap between your current salary and the compensation you want, it's better not to divulge your current salary. For instance, if you're making $80,000 and you want $120,000 a year, even hiring managers at good companies will automatically become defensive and try to negotiate downward. However, if you decide you need to tell them what you are currently making, just make sure that you can justify to them why you are looking for such a large increase. It could be as simple as letting them know that you are speaking to other companies, and this is the range that they are offering.

One other benefit of testing the waters with regard to salary is that over time you develop more confidence. After you've pushed the limit a few times with companies you're only marginally interested in, you will feel more comfortable negotiating with companies that are at the top of your list.

Chapter 6

WRITE A RESUME THAT GETS YOU INTERVIEWS

The goal of a resume is to get you an interview.

But did you know that most recruiters and hiring managers spend only 15 to 30 seconds reviewing each resume, and that they look first for reasons to *disqualify* the candidate? It's no wonder many qualified candidates get passed over. In this chapter, I'll tell you how to keep this from happening to you.

Ineffective Resumes

Many resumes I receive as a recruiter are ineffective. They don't accurately describe the candidate's experience in a manner that matches the job's requirements, and they don't clearly spell out the candidate's accomplishments and capabilities.

Before I submit resumes to hiring managers, I ask a large percentage of candidates to rewrite them, so they are tailored to the job description.

Or I might ask them to write a letter highlighting their most significant professional accomplishments, so the hiring manager can get a full picture of the skills they bring to the table.

The Risk of Not Having a Good Resume

While I was working on a senior-level position that was tough to fill, I found a candidate who seemed like a good fit. I sent the resume over to the hiring manager, but he said he wasn't ready to interview the candidate because he didn't think he was a good fit.

A week later, I told this hiring manager that I didn't have any more candidates, and I asked him if he wanted to interview the one whose resume I had previously sent. He replied that he would like to wait and see if we can find any other candidates who might be more qualified. Another two weeks went by, and we still didn't have any more candidates, so he agreed to interview the one I had mentioned to him.

Here is what this hiring manager wrote about to me after the interview:

> "I was very impressed by Mr. Jones. After interviewing him, I realized he was a much better fit for this position than I was led to believe by his resume. He has a strong background in what I am looking for, and he is very familiar with the type of work that he would need to accomplish in order to be successful. He also struck me as a very intelligent person who would be an asset to have on my team."

By the way, this candidate was able to negotiate a salary of $150,000, and a $5,000 sign-on bonus, but think about how much work it took to make that interview happen. The hiring manager almost didn't interview him because his resume did not reflect the experience that the manager was looking for and thought would be listed out on the resume of a well-qualified candidate. What if another less-proactive recruiter had handled this position? Almost certainly, this candidate would have slipped through the cracks.

> ### Tip
>
> Customize your resume to match the job description, so anyone who gives it thirty seconds will be able to see how it fits the position. Step back and put yourself in the seat of the hiring manager. What information would you be looking for? Make sure that information is in your resume.

Another Real-Life Example

While working at a recruiting agency, I passed the resume of a senior Java software developer to a manager who was seeking to hire such a person. I never heard back from this manager, so I assumed he wasn't interested in this candidate.

About a week later, this manager sent me an e-mail asking for more resumes. I sent him two new ones, along with the first resume once more. Again, I received no response.

A week later, the hiring manager sent me an e-mail asking for more resumes. I didn't have any new ones, so I sent the same resume once again. Within minutes, I got a phone call from the hiring manager. He said, "You've sent me this resume three times. He's not good enough; I need someone with more hands-on experience."

I contacted the candidate, who informed me that he had lots of hands-on experience writing code. I notified the hiring manager, who agreed to interview him on the following Monday. By Friday, he was hired as the architect for one of the company's important software development projects.

Because this candidate failed to tailor his resume to the job, he almost didn't get an interview. If I had been less proactive, the hiring manager almost certainly would have passed him over.

Steps in Building a Great Resume

1. Understand the job

Take a look at the partial job description on the following page. Don't worry if you don't understand all the acronyms. I certainly don't, and most recruiters probably don't either. That's why key words are so important for matching resumes to job descriptions.

Job Description for System Engineer

We are looking for a system engineer to migrate and update our current Active Directory and Exchange to the most recent release. We need someone who can create test plans and create a pilot program to be run in a lab environment to test the upgraded system before it is put into production.

The ideal candidate will also have experience creating and testing Group Polices as well as WSUS, SMS, and SCCM. He or she will also have experience implementing, testing, and de-bugging servers, switches, and SAN products as well as other technologies.

How I Would Review Resumes Submitted for This Job

The job description clearly states that the company is looking for someone with Active Directory and Exchange experience along with experience in several other technologies. The candidate also should have experience with upgrades and migrations.

Here's how I would have searched for candidates for this job using job boards, LinkedIn, and the company's resume database:

- Geographic area: Within a 25 to 30 mile radius

- Job title: System Engineer

- Key Words: "Active Directory," "Exchange," and then possibly "upgrade" or "migration" or "implementation."

    Candidates who did not use these key words on their resume would be filtered out. I could have listed additional keywords (this is commonly done), but that might have eliminated too many qualified candidates. My personal preference is to cast a wide net and then drill down.

Sometimes, a hiring manager may specify that a specific skill set or technology must be in the resume. I will then search using that key word, which will disqualify all candidates who do not use it, even though they might be qualified.

Portions of Actual Resume Submitted by the Successful Candidate

Note how the resume is tailored to the job description.

> **Title:** System Engineer
>
> **Experience:** As a System Engineer, I recently completed an Active Directory and Exchange upgrade and implementation project for over 45,000 users. The systems were upgraded from the 2000 platform to the 2008 platform. During this project, I was responsible for creating and de-bugging the WSUS, SMS, SCCM as well as Group Policies.
>
> I also built out and tested the switches, servers, and storage products for use on the LAN and WAN. And I tested the solutions in a lab, which I created, and I would run them through a pilot program before we would put them into production.

This candidate's resume almost perfectly mirrored the job description. Most importantly, he mentioned which versions of the software he had worked on and the scope of the project. This indicates that he probably possesses a high level of technical ability. He probably copied the format of his resume from the job description, which is fine. Any hiring manager would be foolish to ignore this candidate.

This candidate did another thing right. He listed the most relevant experience at the top of his resume, under his current job, so people reading the resume would have their attention captured right off the bat.

How I Review Resumes

Because of the large amount of resumes I have to review on a daily basis and because of the limited amount of time in a day, the first thing I do when reviewing a resume is to try and find a way to disqualify it from consideration. Here are the steps I typically follow, with the approximate times I devote to each:

- **Geographic area:** Does the candidate live in the immediate area? Although some positions and some companies may allow for relocation, most don't. If out of the area, I will stop reading. (3 seconds).

- **Match job description?** If not a match, I will stop reading. (7 seconds).

- **Job hopper?** I eliminate candidates who have held multiple positions for under a year or numerous positions within a few years. (3 seconds).

- **Gaps in their employment history?** If any gaps, I scratch the candidate. (3 seconds)

- **Appropriate experience?** If the resume is still alive, I will go back and take a closer look at the actual experience to decide if the candidate is a good match. (15 seconds)

If the resume has made it through all of the above steps, I will reach out to the candidate.

Why Recruiters May Pass on Candidates Who Present a Risk

Once, I sent a resume to a hiring manager on behalf of a candidate who seemed to perfectly fit the job. However, because he had a gap in his employment history, the manager refused to interview him. When I inquired why, he told me, "He was unemployed, so there must be something wrong with him."

Candidates who are job hoppers or have gaps in their employment history present risks. Most recruiters prefer to pass over risky candidates rather than risk their reputations. Unhappy hiring managers are likely to complain to the recruiter's boss and even higher. I've seen hiring managers complain to CEOs of billion-dollar companies that they are not getting the recruiting support they expect. That is why a recruiter isn't going to take a risk on sending over someone who may not be a fit. Even if a recruiter thinks a somewhat risky candidate might be a fit, he may decide to play it safe and ignore the resume.

Common Resume Mistakes that Can Disqualify a Candidate

- **Spelling:** I have known many hiring managers who would pass over candidates who had as few as two words misspelled on their resume. I don't blame them. Spelling errors can indicate lack of attention to detail, lack of motivation, and other deficiencies.

- **Contact info:** I receive at least one resume a month that lacks contact information or has incorrect or misspelled contact information. I just delete these. Some people put their work e-mail and work phone number on their resume, which is fine if you also include your regular e-mail and phone number. Your resume will be deposited into a resume database, and a recruiter may try to reach out to you in the future to see if you might be interested in a great opportunity. If you are no longer at that old e-mail or phone number, we will have no way of getting in touch with you.

- **Key words:** If your resume does not have the proper key words, it might get passed over by the search engine, even if you are a great fit for the position. For example, if you are a software engineer specializing in Java, and you don't have the word Java in your resume, then your resume won't surface in a search on that term.

Real-Life Example

When I was a recruiter in a large company, someone in a hiring manager's business unit recommended a candidate for a position we were seeking to fill. Because this candidate's resume did not contain any of the desired key words, and it wasn't tailored to the job, the hiring manager didn't want to bring him in for an interview. He finally agreed to do so, however, since the candidate was a personal referral. It turned out that this candidate did have the relevant experience, and he soon had a job offer in hand. If that candidate's friend hadn't been there to vouch for him, we would have passed on him because his resume didn't match the job description. And if I had to search for a resume to fill this position his resume wouldn't have popped up when I did my search because his resume did not contain any of the key words that the job required.

Tip

Most search engines in job boards and in company databases pull the most relevant and most recent resumes to the top, using key words as the primary criteria. Some even show how many times each key word is used. Busy recruiters slow down and read resumes that have lots of matching key words, so the more key words the better. If there is a particular company that you are interested in working for, it's good to go back into their system on a regular basis to either update your resume or apply for another job. This will keep your resume is fresh. Most of the candidates I have hired from a company resume database have applied to other positions within the company during the past year or years.

More Tips for Writing Winning Resumes

- **Clarity:** Make your resume clear and easy to ready. Avoid italic type; it is more difficult to read.

- **Length:** I get this question from candidates all the time. Don't worry about the length of your resume. Three pages or less is fine. Just make sure it is as concise as possible. Recruiters and hiring managers don't like to wade through unnecessary information. Your most recent experience is going to be the most important, so include the most detail in this area. Of course, if you are an entry-level candidate or just beginning your career, it's best to have your resume on one page.

- **Education**: If you went to a highly reputable school, I recommend putting educational information near the top of your resume. This is also wise if you are short on work experience. Anyone with a connection to that school or who has a favorable impression of that institution might give your resume more attention.

Customizing Your Resume

To make sure your resume gets read, do the following:

- Read the job description and make a list of what experiences and skills you think the hiring manager wants to see.

- Include these experiences in your resume.

- Quantify your experiences and accomplishments as much as possible to demonstrate that you have the experience to do the job.

- Review the resume as if you are the hiring manager. What would a hiring manager or a recruiter reviewing your resume for 15-30 seconds be likely to notice? How well does your stated experience match the needs of the position?

- Make sure that your most recent experience (last 3 to 5 years) relates to the job description. If that experience looks good, then most recruiters will slow down and read the rest.

Building a Resume

To help you understand how to develop good resume content, we'll go through some exercises involving a few different types of jobs.

Job Title: Help Desk Technician

What qualities will a hiring manager and recruiter look for in a candidate for this job? Probably the following:

- Good customer service skills
- Experience tracking customer service issues
- Able to handle numerous calls every day
- Specific technical skills required

Let's look at part of a resume of a candidate who got a job doing helpdesk:

Company X   August 2008–Present
Title: Help Desk Technician

- Gave technical support to customers over the phone and by e-mail to answer questions and help fix computer issues as they related to software, hardware, and peripherals.
- Expert knowledge of MS Windows and related products and operating systems, as well as printers, networks, and blackberry devices.
- Member of the help desk team that supported a large company of over 20,000 employees.
- Handled up to 100 calls and emails a day for customer technical support.
- Used Remedy to open, track, and close technical support requests.
- Won the annual "Best Customer Support" award twice during my three years of employment.

Positives

- The candidate has good job stability.
- The hiring manager can see he has experience handling a lot of calls every day at a large company and is probably very familiar with all sorts of tech support requests.

- He has shown that he uses Remedy to track all customer support requests.

- And most importantly, within the three years he has been working at that company, he won best customer support twice.

What could he have done better?

The only suggestion I might have is to describe in more detail what specific technologies he has experience supporting. Some of this information is included, but if the hiring manager had said he only wanted to see candidates with experience in certain technologies, this candidate might have been passed over. Nevertheless, this resume is good enough to cause me to slow down and take a closer look.

Another Winning Resume

Here's another example of part of a resume of someone who got a job as an executive assistant to the CEO of a large, publicly held company. If you were the hiring manager, what would catch your eye? If you saw just this portion of the resume, would you slow down and review the resume in greater detail?

Company Y   October 2005–Present
Executive Assistant

- Provided administrative support to the CEO of a $800 million dollar publicly held company.

- Handled heavy calls and acted as a gatekeeper for the CEO.

- Responsible for setting up all executive-level meetings and preparing meeting agendas.

- Responsible for arranging travel, including car rental, airline reservations, and hotel reservations, as well as preparing and submitting expense reports.

What caught your eye right away?

- I immediately noticed that for more than six years she was an executive assistant to a CEO for an $800 million dollar publicly held company. That would indicate that she has a full understanding of what the job entails. Her length of service in that position leads me to believe that she is pretty good at her job and is probably worth considering as a candidate.

Another Example of Part of a Resume

Review this resume and ask yourself whether you think this person can do the job:

Company X   July 2007–Present
Sales Executive

As a sales executive at Company X, I was responsible for selling enterprise software solutions to Fortune 1000 companies.

- Achieved 220% of a $1.5 million quota.

- Ranked #2 out of 30 sales representatives.

- Made 50 cold calls a day and would set up a minimum of 5 in-person meetings a week with C-level decision makers in Fortune 1000 companies.

- Turned around an underperforming territory into one of the best.

- Closed deals averaging $75,000, with the largest being $450,000.

The above resume indicates an ability to sell, but does this experience relate to the position he is applying for? If so, he'll probably get called in for an interview. His best bet is to focus his job hunting on direct competitors or on companies that will view his experience as an asset.

Content Is King

Recruiters and hiring managers won't spend a lot of time looking at your resume, so content is far more important than format. Most recruiters don't care whether your resume is nicely laid out or is on thick pink paper. Besides, when you apply to a job on a company's website, your resume will enter into an applicant tracking system which may reformat it. Often, the reformatted version is harder to read!

To develop content for your resume, answer the following questions:

- What were your major accomplishments and did you quantify those results?

- What goals did your manager set for you? Quantify how you exceeded those results.

- What were your daily responsibilities?

- Do all of the above answers relate to the position you are applying for?

- If not, can you tailor your experience, so it mirrors the job description you are applying for?

I didn't include any complete sample resumes in this book because it's more important to focus on content. To see some sample formatted resumes, go to my website or do a quick Google search. The most important thing is to ensure that your experience matches the job's requirements and that you have quantified that experience and your accomplishments. That will greatly improve your chances of getting an interview and getting hired!

Chapter 7

WRITE A COVER LETTER
THAT MAKES
YOU STAND OUT

In my role as a professional recruiter, I've noticed these days that very few job candidates send cover letters with their resumes. When I do see a cover letter, I usually glance at it for only a second or two. That's because most are so poorly written that they're a waste of time to read, which means they were a waste of time to write.

That doesn't need to be the case. Indeed, it shouldn't be. A well-written cover letter can be a powerful tool. It will grab the attention of recruiters and hiring managers and cause them to want to read your resume. In fact, I've known job candidates to get an interview *primarily* because they sent a cover letter along with their resume.

What makes a good cover letter? I'll answer that question by showing you two actual cover letters that came across my desk. First, here's one example of what not to do:

To Whom It May Concern,

I am a seasoned, results-generating individual with experience in finance, accounting, and operations. I have proven success in different areas, including legal, policy, and administration, as well as Sarbanes Oxley. I also have experience in developing reports and presenting them to the executive team.

I am an intuitive and proven leader who is great at building and maintaining productive relationships with clients and collaborating with them, as well as with my peers. And I also have great communication skills.

As I read this cover letter, these were my thoughts:

1. What does this candidate mean when he says he is "seasoned"? Is he seasoned with salt and pepper? Fresh herbs? Sour cream n' chives? He's making me hungry, and my mind has moved on to other things.

2. He says he is "results generating," yet he doesn't tell me what results he has produced. Quantifying some of his accomplishments in bullet-point format would have grabbed my attention.

3. He then goes on to mention that he has had "proven success in different areas." What successes and what areas? I have no clue what challenges he has faced, what he had to do to overcome them, or what end results he achieved.

4. He talks about "developing reports and presenting them to the executive team." What reports did he develop? Why were they important? What did the company gain from his efforts? How does this relate to the job he is applying for?

5. He says he is an "intuitive and proven leader." What does this mean? Is he psychic? If he can read people's minds, that would be

impressive. But kidding aside, I really might be impressed if he had cited his specific accomplishments as a team leader.

6. Finally, he mentions that he is great at building and maintaining relationships and collaborating with others. I certainly hope so. Otherwise, he'd have trouble holding any job. In fact, I have never had any job applicant admit to being a poor team player.

What did I learn about this person from reading this cover letter? Absolutely nothing! In fact, in two seconds, I determined that this cover letter wasn't worth reading and decided that the candidate's resume probably wouldn't be worth reading either. This cover letter actually did this candidate more harm than good.

On the other hand, if this person had told me specifically what he had accomplished and how his qualifications and accomplishments related to the job I was seeking to fill, I would have been very interested in reading his resume. I want to see quantified facts, not boastful generalities.

Here's an example of a good cover letter:

Hi Jim,

I am a recruiting manager at XYZ Company, and I am very interested in interviewing for the job opening you have for a recruiting manager. Some of my successes include

- Managing a team of eight recruiters who hired more than 300 candidates a year.

- Reducing time-to-hire from 40 days to 29 days, resulting in an annual savings to the company of $550,000.

- Restructuring my team to achieve maximum efficiency by allowing each recruiter to focus on sourcing for candidates based on specific skill sets.

As you can see from my enclosed resume, I have more than eleven years of successful experience in recruiting. I would welcome the opportunity to speak with you in person.

Yours truly,

What did this person do right?

- This cover letter is concise and filled with facts. It will pique the interest of the busiest recruiter or executive.

- This candidate took the trouble to find out the recruiter's name and personalize the letter.

- He does not simply mention that he is a "proven leader" or that he has "proven success." He demonstrates that he has been successful by quantifying his accomplishments and describing the size of his team.

- In this case, working for XYZ Company was a significant selling point because it possessed a strong brand, and it happened to be a direct competitor of the hiring company. A successful track record in a company with a business model similar to the one where you want to work can be a huge plus. You'll be viewed as a less risky hire, which means that your chances of getting the job will be significantly greater.

One or two additional bullet points would have made this cover letter even stronger. However, as written, it helped win this candidate an interview.

Let's take a look at an example of an entry-level cover letter.

Hi Sarah,

I came across your profile on LinkedIn and saw that you graduated from New York University in computer science. I am about to graduate from NYC, also with a degree in computer science, and I wanted to see if you might be able to give me some guidance in my job search.

- I currently have a 3.7 GPA.
- Last summer, I interned as a Java developer at Company Y, a social media startup, where I worked as a member of a project team that used Java and J2EE to create new features for the company's website.
- I am fluent in C/C++, HTML, Javascript, Perl, PHP, and SQL.

I've attached my resume for you to review. Would you like to schedule a time to talk, possibly next Wednesday or Thursday at 10 a.m.?

Best regards,

Michelle

What did this candidate do well and not so well?

- **Well:** She effectively used this cover letter to reach out to someone for advice, which is a low-pressure way of networking and possibly getting an interview. She also improved her chances of connecting with this person by calling attention to their mutual connections (same department at the same university).

- **Not so well:** She could have done a better job of describing her internship. It probably gave her some really good experience, and she should have gone into greater detail about the project and her responsibilities.

    For example, if her internship had been with Facebook, she might have said something like this:

    "When I interned at Facebook, I was part of an eight-person team that developed a new application. It allows users to subscribe to the posts of others with the option of receiving all of their posts or only the most important. We were able to complete this project on schedule in eight weeks. Near the end of my internship, I had the proud pleasure of watching the company roll out this new application to all of its 800 million users."

In this hypothetical example of a cover letter, the candidate gives people a good idea of what she did and how much work was involved. If you are unable to convey this degree of quantifiable success in your resume and cover letter, don't sell yourself short. Use your own work experience, whatever that is, to demonstrate what you know and what you are capable of accomplishing.

A Cover Letter Can Help You Stand Out: A Real-Life Example

Some time ago, I was working for a company that was experiencing explosive growth. To staff a new business unit, we needed to hire more than 100 people. We held a job fair to offer the positions first to our employees, and about fifty qualified candidates showed up for interviews.

After the interviews, I sat down with the management team to go over each resume and review our notes. As I passed out the resumes one by one to the managers and announced each candidate's name, one name elicited a universally favorable response. The managers all remembered this candidate as the only one whose resume was accompanied by a cover letter.

The management team appreciated the extra effort this candidate had made, and they offered him a job. I can't say for sure that the cover letter got him the job, but it certainly made him stand out in a very helpful way. Thus, it never hurts to write a cover letter, and it could make a big difference.

A Real-Life Example of What Not to Do

I received one cover letter that actually diminished the applicant's chances of getting a job. He started by telling me that he went to high school in New Jersey and graduated in 1991. He lost my interest right there.

He went on to tell me that "he thinks tactically, strategically, and has a tendency to study human behavior." I immediately thought, so do stalkers and serial killers, but that doesn't mean we are going to hire them. Then he wrote, "I think I can accomplish great things." Good grief! I want to know what you have accomplished, not that you think you can accomplish great things.

Good cover letters are worth the investment. When candidates cite their specific and relevant accomplishments, I'm much more likely to put them in front of hiring managers. I'll go out of my way to help candidates find employment when they have sold me on their value to the company. To do this, they have to make it clear what they have achieved and how their skills and experience could benefit our company. A cover letter can help achieve this objective.

Recruiters and hiring managers often have hundreds of resumes to review. A well-written cover letter will make your resume stand out from the stack, so it actually gets read. I know this to be true from my own experience and from talking to other recruiting professionals. In fact, there have been times when I considered passing on candidates until I noticed their cover letters highlighting their accomplishments. And because of that I wound up reading those resumes, and some of those candidates were eventually hired.

Keep in mind the purpose of the cover letter is to whet the appetite of recruiters and hiring managers, so they will want to read your resume. And, while a poorly written cover letter is a waste of time, a well-written one is a powerful tool that can give you the edge over the competition.

To create content for a cover letter, review the questions I posed to develop content for a resume at the end of the last chapter. And yes, it's okay if some of the information on your resume ends up on your cover letter.

Chapter 8

WORK YOUR NETWORK

Whether you know it or not, you have a network. That network is powerful. It can help you, and it also can seriously harm you. In this chapter, we'll talk about both sides of networking, so you can take advantage of the benefits and guard against the threats. Let's discuss the negative side first.

The Dark Side of Networks

Did you know that companies can eliminate you from consideration for a job before you even interview and never tell you why? It happens all the time. When it does, it may be because some bit of detrimental information has found its way to the person doing the hiring.

Like it or not, your reputation follows you wherever you go. The primary communications channel for your reputation is your network. It consists of your present and former employers and co-workers, your friends, fellow members of organizations, and virtually every person you know or have known. In fact, people who don't even know you, but only know *about* you are also in your network.

I want to let you in on one of the dirty little secrets of the hiring process. It's called the "back door reference check." A back door reference check means a hiring manager plans to secretly check up on a candidate. The candidate has no idea who will be contacted as a reference or even that this reference checking is underway. And to make matters worse, the information the company gathers could be completely inaccurate.

A Real-Life Example

A candidate I once submitted to a position seemed like an ideal candidate, but he didn't get the job. The hiring manager later told me that he was about to make an offer, but at the last minute, he changed his mind because of back-door information he received about this person. Maybe this negative information was inaccurate, but it created doubts in the minds of the company's management, and they didn't want to take a risk. This is an example of the negative power of networks.

It's not unusual for hiring managers to tell me things like this:

- "I've been warned by someone not to hire this person. I'll pass."

- "I have heard some things about this person from someone who used to work with him that concerns me, and I will pass on him."

Here is an e-mail I actually received from a co-worker:

> "I've heard that a John Doe has (or may be) contacting you regarding a job. I want to give you a heads up about him. I worked with him in company X for three years. He not only was incompetent in his job, he showed great lack of moral character. This guy is serious bad news. I am also certain that anyone else who has worked with him will agree."

Another Real-Life Experience

One of my co-workers sent a candidate on an interview. The candidate accepted the job offer and put in her two-week's notice. On the Friday before the Monday she was supposed to start her new job, someone told the hiring manager that he had heard that the new hire was difficult to work with. The hiring manager pulled the offer that very day. It's pretty sad that they left this person out in the cold. But this type of thing happens, and candidates are never told exactly why.

What others think of us can be skewed because of their own personal issues and biases. I once had two people come to me, each complaining that the other was hateful and incompetent. Obviously, both needed to examine their own attitudes and behaviors, but they preferred to blame the other person. What if one of these people pursued a new position? The other, if consulted, would probably have given a damaging reference, and the candidate would never know.

It's pretty difficult to get along with every single person you work with. There will always be people who are liable to give you a poor reference. As a person looking for a job, you need to be alert for people in your network who might sabotage your career, so you can do everything possible to smooth out those relationships.

When hiring, you need to remember that feedback about a person can be inaccurate. You never know what each individual's situation is at any given company. Someone might not be performing well currently, but in another company or situation this person could blossom.

Another Real-Life Story

A while back, I sent several people from the same company to interview for a job. One after another, they were rejected. The hiring manager told me the reason was the poor references he was receiving through the back door. Finally, I completely stopped sending people from that particular company. I just couldn't bear to get them excited about a position, knowing that I would probably have to call them back and tell them that that "the hiring team had decided to go in a different direction." These people never knew the real reason they didn't get the job, and I never found out who was passing on this negative feedback.

The Benefits of Networks

Now that you know how your reputation can prevent you from getting a job, let's focus on how it can help you get a job. Previously, I mentioned that companies can easily get 50 percent of their hires from employee referrals. Some companies pay $1,000 to $3,000 or even more for a successful referral. The vast majority of these referrals come from employees in the company who are recommending people they used to work with.

As I have said, whether you know it or not, you already have a network, and one of your strongest networks consists of your co-workers. If you stay with a big company for a few years, chances are some of your co-workers have already left and are working for direct competitors, some of which might be companies where you might someday want to work. Furthermore, some of your co-workers probably have worked at companies you would consider working for.

Your network of present and past co-workers can be a terrific source of information about companies of interest to you, and many will even offer to introduce you to key individuals. Even if they haven't worked at a specific company, they may know someone who has. As I mentioned previously, this happened to me when one of my old co-workers introduced me to a friend of hers who in turn gave me helpful information about employment in Silicon Valley. This referral was even willing to open up her network to me and introduce me to hiring managers.

Beyond Your Co-workers

Co-workers are often the primary network for referrals, but they're certainly not the only one. How about your 1,248 friends you have on Facebook, for example? Certainly, there must be someone among them who has knowledge about getting a job at a company you admire. If you are an entry-level candidate, perhaps you can get guidance from a friend who graduated ahead of you. Or maybe one of your Facebook friends has a relative or a friend who might be able to help you with referrals.

Don't overlook your old high school friends. I've actually contacted several, most of whom I hadn't spoken with in years, to see what information they had about certain companies. Sometimes, parents and relatives are a good source of contacts or even jobs. Nepotism can be tricky, but it can also work well if the chemistry is right.

Building Your Network

You should constantly be cultivating and building your network. Here are some ideas about how to do that:

- Ask your co-workers to introduce you to people they know really well. Even if you aren't looking for a job, it's smart to research the market, so you have a good idea of what you are worth and what it is like to work at certain companies. After you talk with people, send thank you notes and add them to your LinkedIn account.

- Contact people through LinkedIn, or by e-mail or phone, and ask them if they would be willing to talk to you for a few minutes and give you some career advice. One of my favorite questions is, "What company did you like working for best and why?" If you reach out to people politely and respectfully, and you don't specifically ask for a job, most will get back to you. Later, after you've established a relationship, you might be able to share your credentials and ask for help. If you're currently job hunting, you might ask them if they know any company that is hiring people with your background. They might be able to point you in the right direction.

> **TIP**
>
> When reaching out to people you don't know, it helps to have something in common. Often, attending the same university can establish immediate rapport. Most universities have online alumni associations that help graduates get in touch with each other. Alumni meetings are great places to network as well. You never know who you will meet. One of my friends met her husband at one!

- Classes are a good place to network. I've made some good contacts (and good friends) through postgraduate/continuing education classes at universities. Any type of class, even martial arts or yoga, can afford networking opportunities.

- Charity events are good places to meet people, especially when you work side-by-side with people on a project.

- User groups and conferences are fruitful sources of contacts for certain fields of work, such as information technology.

- Meetup.com is a great website that allows members to connect with other members who have similar interests or who wish to attend group functions or events.

Target Networking

The most efficient way to network is to target people who work at a company or in the industry that interests you. Social media makes it easy to gather this type of intelligence. For example, search LinkedIn for the names of a few hiring managers who work for a company you would like to approach. Use Google to collect information about their activities. For example, perhaps someone you would like to meet is scheduled to speak at a conference you might attend. If not speaking, check meetup.com to see if this person is registered to attend a particular outing or event.

If you go to an event with the purpose of meeting someone, of course you don't just say, "Hi! I'm John Doe, and I would like to work for you." Do some research online to see what common interests you share. When you "bump" into this person, know what you want to ask. Suggest that you meet at another time for coffee, drinks, or a meal. Exchange business cards and perhaps agree to connect on LinkedIn.

This type of networking really works. As a recruiter, hiring managers often send me resumes of people they met at conferences or workshops. If you put some time into building your network, it will serve you well.

Chapter 9

UNDERSTAND HOW RECRUITERS FIND YOUR RESUME

most job applicants don't understand how the online recruitment process works. They simply post their resume online or apply for a job online and hope for the best. You can waste a lot of time and effort with that approach, and you may never find the job you're looking for.

The purpose of this chapter is to remove the mystery from the online applying and posting process, so that you can understand how it works and hopefully realize that this is just one of many tools you can use to help you in your job search. Different recruiters operate differently, but it will be helpful for you to know how I operated when I was a recruiter for a large company.

When I received a new job opening that was open to external candidates, I immediately posted it on our career website, so people could apply. Then, I would conduct a search in our resume database and reach out to all qualified candidates. If it appeared the position was going to be tough to fill, I would post it online to job boards, such as Monster.com, Careerbuilder.com, Dice, and LinkedIn. If I still couldn't find a qualified candidate, I would log onto one of these job boards and conduct a search in their resume database.

You as a job seeker could be competing against hundreds of candidates for one position, based solely on the strength of your resume. Not only do you need to have an impressive resume, but your qualifications need to match the needs of the job. What's more, your success at connecting with a job depends on the effectiveness of the recruiter. Some un-alert recruiters might pass over resumes that are perfect. Others may lack clarity about what the hiring manager is looking for.

Why Recruiters May Overlook Your Resume

I was once asked to take over for another recruiter who had been trying to fill a certain job position for more than two months. The hiring manager was getting frustrated because the recruiter was unable to find her any qualified candidates. I looked over all 116 candidates who had applied, and I was shocked to find ten who seemed to be a perfect fit. When I sent their resumes to the hiring manager, she wanted to interview all of them. But by this time, many were no longer available.

The recruiter I replaced had more than five years of experience in recruiting, and yet she had no clue what she was looking for. This situation is not unusual. When you apply for a job, don't assume that your resume is in good hands. Exercise personal initiative and come up with strategic ways to approach your target companies. I'll go over some of these techniques in upcoming chapters.

Sometimes, recruiters are simply too busy to give your resume the attention it deserves. Once, when I was trying to fill several positions for a huge project, I was so overloaded with candidates that for several months I simply stopped considering new applicants. If the perfect candidate had applied for one of these positions, no one would have noticed. I wasn't reviewing new resumes because I didn't have time, and I already had enough candidates.

Another thing worth knowing is if you apply to more than one position at a given company, the recruiter who finds your resume first may exercise exclusive rights to it. In other words, you will only be considered for the job being handled by that one recruiter.

Phantom Jobs

Occasionally, companies advertise positions that don't exist. That sounds ridiculous, but it can happen when companies want to build a reservoir of candidates. This might especially occur when they're bidding on a contract they hope to win or when they have a continuing need for candidates with the same sets of skills.

The way job boards bill for their services encourages this practice. Most companies enter into agreements with the job boards to purchase a specific number of job postings per month. For example, if a company has paid for five postings, and it has only three jobs to fill, it must decide what to do with the other two available postings. If they don't use them, they lose them. Rather than "waste" the money, some companies will use the extra postings to advertise fictitious positions to fill their pipelines.

Some recruiters keep old jobs on the job boards after they've been filled because they're too lazy to take them down. Even though some jobs that are posted on company career sites or on job boards aren't real, it still never hurts to apply. Most of the time, your resume and contact information will go into the company's recruiting database. Sometime in the future, possibly years later when the stars are perfectly aligned, you might be contacted about the perfect job!

When I was working as a recruiter for a large company, I found the majority of my candidates through the company's resume database. In fact, virtually everyone I recruited at one time or another had applied to our company. While at that job, I rarely used job boards like Monster.com and Careerbuilder.com.

Applying for Jobs

Jobs posted by companies with outstanding reputations will attract a large number of resumes, many of which will come from unqualified candidates. When I say "unqualified," I mean candidates who have absolutely no business applying for that job. You would be surprised at how many teachers, plumbers, and carpenters apply for software development or analyst positions. And yes, I have even received a few resumes from exotic dancers.

These days, I'm pleased if I get one or two good candidates per job posting. To glean the few good ones, I have to wade through a stack of poor resumes. As I mentioned in one of the earlier chapters, I typically give each resume a fifteen-second glance to try to spot reasons to disqualify it from consideration. If the resume passes this initial screening and meets certain basic criteria (e.g., geographic location, skills, and employment history), I'll take a closer look.

Because so many unqualified candidates apply for jobs, recruiters might spend less time looking over candidates who apply for a job online and more time proactively searching for candidates in our resume database and online. We are more likely to come across the right candidate for the position with this approach because we can search by skills, key words, and other relevant criteria.

At large companies, each recruiter can easily have twenty or more open positions at any one time. If each position is posted somewhere online, and the average posting brings in a few resumes a day, you can imagine how much time this recruiter must spend reviewing resumes, on top of handling a host of other daily tasks. Because job postings produce so few good candidates, you can see why many recruiters consider reviewing these postings a waste of time. Instead, they spend most of their time searching their database, job boards, and social media websites. Some even make cold calls to candidates.

> **Tip**
>
> You only need to apply once for each position. Applying for the same position three times isn't going to improve your chances of getting an interview. It's only going to frustrate the recruiter. By the way, anytime you apply for a position, the appropriate recruiter is usually notified. If you seem like a fit, you will be contacted.

Posting Your Resume Online

As I mentioned earlier, sometimes it's easier to get a position with a company if you post your resume online instead of applying directly to the company.

When you post your resume online, make sure it is clear and easy to read. Follow all the rules I mentioned earlier. Include all the key words a recruiter might use to search for your resume. You could get passed over if the right words are absent from your resume.

> **Tip**
>
> Every recruiter wants to be first to reach out to new candidates. When they come in on Monday mornings, they immediately look over the online databases to see if any new candidates posted their resume over the weekend. For this reason, I recommend posting your resume on a Sunday night.

Keeping Your Resume Fresh

If you are a qualified candidate with skills that are in demand, you will get a lot of calls from corporate and agency recruiters during the first week after posting your resume online. As the days go by, your chances of being contacted by a recruiter decrease considerably. If the calls stop before you've found the right job, take your resume offline for a day, a week, or a month. When you repost it later, it will look fresh. Or see if the job board you are using has a refresh feature that will do the same thing without having to take your resume offline.

The reason for this is recruiters compete for candidates, and they don't want to waste their time contacting candidates whom they assume have already been contacted by other recruiters. Agency recruiters get paid when they place candidates, and only the first recruiter who refers a candidate to a job will get a commission. That's why recruiters are always going after "fresh meat."

Confidentiality

Most of the job boards offer a feature that allows you to keep your resume confidential. This means that potential employers can see your resume and not your name and contact information. Interested recruiters and hiring managers must e-mail an anonymous e-mail address to contact you.

As a recruiter, I've had bad experiences with "confidential" postings, and I don't think I'm alone. I have e-mailed many of these candidates, and not one has ever responded. I've concluded that trying to contact these candidates is a waste of time, and I no longer bother. If you really want a job, I strongly advise against this approach. One safe approach, however, is to post your resume on LinkedIn. Since it's viewed more as a social networking tool, no one will think twice about it. I will go into more detail about this later.

Job Boards

There are multiple major job boards on the market these days, as well as hundreds of niche sites, and new job boards seem to be popping up all the time. However, not all companies subscribe to every job board.

At the main job boards like Monster, CareerBuilder, and Dice, it can cost companies on average $10,000 a year for a single recruiter to be able to search the resume database nationwide. And that doesn't include the cost of a job posting. As you can imagine, companies are going to restrict their subscriptions to the job boards that work best for them. That's why some really good jobs may not be posted on some job boards.

However, job boards are still a great tool for you to use, so you can see what other companies might be hiring in your area. As a recruiter who talks to candidates on a daily basis, I am always amazed about how many companies in my local area exist that I have never heard of before. These companies could offer some great opportunities, which is one of the reasons it always pays to keep an eye on the job boards, so you know what other potential opportunities exist.

Job Board Aggregators

Job board aggregators pull job announcements from hundreds of websites, including company career sites, and display them on one website. Some have great functionality that can be extremely useful. The two I recommend are Simplyhired.com and Indeed.com.

LinkedIn

Throughout this book, I've mentioned several ways you can use LinkedIn to maintain and build your network of contacts. You should be aware that LinkedIn also functions very effectively as a job board. Companies can and do post open positions on it, and recruiters and hiring managers often list open positions on their profile page. LinkedIn also has a service that allows recruiters to search, find, and reach out to candidates, just like a standard job board. Plus, you can place your resume on LinkedIn for all to see, without appearing to be in the market for a job.

Because of these and other features, more and more recruiters are using LinkedIn. The vice president of recruiting at a $2.5 billion publicly held company asked the recruiting team which job board they would choose if they could only use one. A friend of mine who works there told me that the unanimous choice was LinkedIn.

Tip

Regularly ask people to recommend you on LinkedIn. When your profile is complete and you have several recommendations, your chances of favorably impressing recruiters and hiring managers increase dramatically.

While plenty of people do find and get jobs by posting their resume online or by applying to a job on a job board or a company career site, personally, I prefer to use these sites as more of a research tool to see what opportunities and companies exist and then reach out to the hiring manager directly. I'll go over some of those techniques in chapter 11.

Chapter 10

KNOW HOW TO WORK WITH RECRUITERS

Once you apply to a position, although a hiring manager might reach out to you directly, you most likely will start working with a recruiter. It's important to know how to work with recruiters because they could be your most powerful ally to help you land your dream job. Some recruiters might even go so far as to share the salary range a position can pay so that you can ask for the most money possible. I know recruiters who when a candidate was asking for a lower salary than what the company could pay and the recruiter knew that candidate was underpaid they coached that candidate on what to ask for. Recruiters might also tell you what to expect in the interview, so you can properly prepare yourself to succeed in the interview.

And while a recruiter might have the ability to help you get the job of your dreams, they also have the power to prevent you from getting a job, even if you are the perfect candidate.

Some people have the misconception that recruiters are "gatekeepers." This is true in some sense, but it isn't completely accurate. For example, many people who apply to our jobs aren't remotely qualified for the position, so, to them, we might be considered a gatekeeper. However, unless their father or uncle ran the company, they aren't ever going to qualify for that position.

And if we are to be considered anything, then I would say we are the "middlemen" who work between two different parties, the hiring manager and the candidate, to negotiate a mutually beneficial agreement. We aren't on Facebook looking for inappropriate pictures that you might have posted with your friends because that's not our job. And if you are having trouble negotiating with us, it's usually because we are following the directive of a hiring manager.

At the end of the day, we are paid to fill positions. Our performance is measured by how many positions we fill and how quickly we fill them. Our job is not to keep qualified candidates out. In fact, we want to find as many qualified candidates as possible in the shortest amount of time because that demonstrates we are doing a good job. And if we believe you are a qualified candidate, many times, we will bend over backwards to do what it takes to bring you on board, so we can move on to the next position.

Now, with all that being said, if you happen to annoy us by over communicating with us or you come across as rude or unprofessional, we aren't going to want to deal with you or help you. Now, you have presented yourself as a potential risk, and you are preventing us from doing our job because of the additional time that you are now taking up.

Throughout this chapter, I will give you some more examples of how to work with recruiters and how not to. However, first, I want to go over the different types of recruiters you may encounter during your job search.

Two Types of Recruiters

1. **Corporate Recruiters.** These types of recruiters either work for the company you are applying to or they contract their services to

that company. Both usually have about the same amount of insight, knowledge, and leverage within the company.

A corporate recruiter's success is measured by how many hires they make. The actual number will differ from each company, but in a big company, it could average around 15 hires a quarter. And some companies tie in a bonus to reward recruiters who make or exceed their goal.

TIP

Chances are if you are interested in a position that a recruiter is working that has been open for a long time or if the recruiter hasn't made many hires that quarter, you might have more leverage in this exchange than they do. You might be able to use that information to get the recruiter to give you more inside information about the job than what they would normally give out, such as the salary range because if you are qualified for the position, they aren't going to want to risk losing you and having to start their search all over again.

---

2. **Agency Recruiters.** The other type of recruiter is the agency recruiter. This recruiter does not work for the company you are trying to get a job at, and they usually have a contract in place where they make money only if they fill the position.

    There are some exceptions with that; for example, if the company is using a true executive recruiter, they will usually pay them a portion of the money upfront, and that recruiting company will get to keep that money whether or not they fill the position.

    Most agency recruiters either place you directly with a company; in which case, they get paid a fee by the company that hired you that could be anywhere from 20 to 33% of your first year's base salary. If it is a high-level position, they might also get that percentage of your bonus as well. For them to collect the money you usually have to stay 3 months or in the case of an executive recruiter, it could be 6 months to a year.

Agency recruiters also hire on a temp-to-hire basis or contract basis. In this case, you become their employee, and they pay you as a contractor, which means you get paid hourly and you do not get benefits or vacation time. So, that means you should be charging a higher hourly rate to make up for that difference. If you get placed on a temp-to-hire position, then usually after 3 or 6 months, you will become an employee of the company you are contracting out too. Then, the company that hires you will pay you salary and benefits, and you probably won't talk to the recruiting agency again.

Agency recruiters are usually either paid a base salary and a commission or a draw and a high commission rate.

Tips:

One thing that I would really like to point out is that some people think very poorly of recruiters. Yes, there are some bad ones out there like there would be in any type of job field, but to help put all this in perspective, recruiters do not work for you.

You do not pay them money, and whether it's a corporate recruiter or an agency recruiter, the company that hires you pays the recruiter. So keep in mind you're not paying them for their time. They are either going to have a job for you right away, in the future, or they are not. Also, if you have broken any of the so-called "unwritten rules" in your career and on your resume (such as job hopping or having some gaps in your employment history), then many recruiters might immediately pass over you because typically hiring managers don't want to hire someone that has had 5 jobs in the last 3 years or hasn't worked in the last 2 years.

You might come across some recruiters who do not return your calls or do not follow up with you once they submit your resume to the hiring manager because they don't want to waste their time telling you that the manager didn't think you were qualified for the position. I do want to caution that some recruiters who work at recruiting agencies might end up wasting your time because the company they work for may make them make so many calls a day, spend so much time on the phone, and bring in so many candidates for face-to-face interviews, and if those numbers aren't met, the recruiter could be fired.

And I have seen plenty of candidates get called in to interview with recruiters at recruiting agencies for positions that do not exist. The recruiter is just scheduling the interview because they are forced to bring in so many candidates every week. That's not a practice I understand.

With that being said, I would like to point out that not every recruiter who works at a recruiting agency is like this, and some of these people might be the most helpful people you will ever find. I just want to point out that some of them might waste your time so that you can look out for that.

How Recruiters Can Help You

Early in my career, I was looking for a new opportunity, and I put my resume on Monster and got a call back from around 10 recruiters who asked me to come in and interview with them and talk to them about some opportunities that they were working on.

I spent a lot of time meeting with those recruiters, and it turned out no one even had a job to send me on. I was pretty frustrated, as you can imagine.

Of course, I ended up finding a job on my own, and about a year later, I was thinking of seeing what else was out there and I called back one of the recruiters, and she actually had 3 great opportunities and 1 of which seemed pretty good. So, she set me up for an interview, and because I had met with her in the past, I didn't have to come back and meet with her again. So, it turned out that time I had spent meeting with her the year before wasn't actually a waste of time after all.

While recruiting agencies might call you in for a position that doesn't exist, keep in mind they do have plenty of positions that do exist, and people get hired into incredible opportunities through them all the time. Plus, they are really great people to have in your network, and you never know when you might need them.

Real-Life Example

I remember when I was working at a company that just went through a round of layoffs. I was told that there weren't going to be any more layoffs, and then, the next day, they had to do another round of layoffs. When that happened, I hit the panic button. I called my recruiter (who worked at a recruiting agency) and placed me at the company I was at, and he was able to get me an interview with the SVP of recruiting for a $2 Billion publicly held company the very next morning at 8 a.m. Now, that is impressive! If I had tried to do that on my own or apply through their website, at best, it might have been a week or so before they probably could have interviewed me, and I would have been interviewing with the hiring manager—not the hiring manager's boss.

So, if you find a few good recruiters, stay in touch with them; you never know when you might need them.

Another good reason to work with agency recruiters is sometimes a company might decide to outsource their positions to an agency recruiter. It might be because they are a small company and they don't have an in-house recruiting team. Or perhaps it's a difficult-to-fill or specialized position or a position that is taking them too long to fill, so they will pass it on to that company to work on. In which case, if you aren't talking to that particular recruiting agency or recruiter, then you might not know about that position.

Working with Recruiters

This should be something that is easy to do and logical, but I am still surprised about how many times good candidates get upset with recruiters or say something negative about them in an interview with the hiring manager.

I have seen this happen multiple times where a candidate will say something bad about the recruiter or the recruiting process. Each time it has happened, the manager makes a strong note about that, and it becomes one of the main reasons that that candidate was not hired.

It's not necessarily that recruiters are great people and that hiring managers have their back, which they do sometimes. It's just that everyone else in the company, including themselves, probably worked with recruiting, and they didn't have a problem with it, and if you are already having problems and complaining about the company's processes, then it might be best to write you off right now because it's obvious that you could be too high maintenance and this could just be the beginning of things to come. And let's be honest; companies are far from perfect, and some of their processes are downright awful; however, as long as you are patient, then you should be able to deal with it.

Keep in mind that if you are working with a corporate recruiter or even an agency recruiter, you do not know what kind of relationship they have with the hiring managers. Most likely corporate recruiters have great working relationships with the hiring managers. They might be sitting right next to them, and they might be dealing with them on a daily basis.

I know that if a candidate starts giving a recruiter a lot of attitude or a hard time, this can have a big influence on whether the person gets hired. Keep in mind there are other reasons why you want to work well with the recruiter.

For starters, they could be your biggest coach and your biggest ally. Most recruiters really do want to help you get that job. Why wouldn't they? They are measured and paid based on the number of people they hire, so they will do a lot for you, more than they are usually asked to do. Plus they know the system and how it works, so they are someone you want on your side.

This is why it pays to cooperate with them. Below you can read about what can happen if you don't cooperate with recruiters.

Real-Life Example

One day I got a call from one of my recruiters who was very sick and could barely talk. She asked me to phone interview a candidate for her and most importantly get the candidate's current salary and desired salary, to which I gladly obliged.

I called the candidate and when I started asking about salary, the candidate went into a long story about why she didn't want to give it out and started telling me this and that. When I asked about her salary expectations, the same thing happened. I went back and tried to ask her a few more times and tried to explain to her that we aren't trying to take anything away from her; the manager just wanted an idea of what she was looking for to see if we could meet her expectations. While the candidate wasn't being mean, she just wasn't cooperating. I got so frustrated with her attitude that I almost hung up on her.

When I got off the phone, I e-mailed my colleague and told her the candidate was being uncooperative at best. My co-worker called me back, and I gave her the full story. Then she said something interesting; she had tried to send the questions to the candidate. For some reason, the candidate didn't want to answer the questions in an e-mail and wanted to talk over the phone. My co-worker agreed that she was being very uncooperative. Actually, she said, "The candidate is being a pain in the ass."

My co-worker never passed that resume on to the hiring manager. It's probably best because it was probably a sign of things to come.

However, the unfortunate thing for the candidate is she spent at least 5 minutes on the phone with me telling me how much she was interested in this position and how badly she wanted it.

All she had to do was tell me what her current salary was and what her expectations were, and she would have been considered. It's too bad because she had a really good resume, but she just wasted our time, talking about this and that and refusing to answer our questions.

And one thing I want to add to all this is there was a time, when you would never talk about salary until the company presented you with an offer.

That time must have come and gone because these days many companies (but not all) want to know those things up front, so they don't waste anyone's time if they can't meet someone's expectations.

Here's Another Example of What Not to Do

I arranged an interview for a candidate and sent him the application to fill out before he arrived. The following is his response back to me:

"I am not going to be able to complete this application before I meet with the team. As we briefly discussed yesterday, we need to have a mutual understanding that I am the right fit for this opportunity and vice versa. I will be happy to fill it out once both parties are convinced that I am the right candidate and this is the right career move for me. We can then move forward with the next steps."

By the way this was an incredibly basic application; it would have taken no more than 5 minutes to complete. I just told the hiring manager that he wasn't filling out the application and cooperating with me, and we canceled the interview and moved on to someone else.

Now let me give you an example of how working with a recruiter can help you get the career of your dreams!

I was working on some positions that were located in Europe. And I had a candidate who was really interested, and he was invited in for an interview. He didn't pass the interview; however, when I looked at his notes, I felt that he was judged unfairly and that he had seemed to have been interviewed for a much higher level position than what he was seeking. Based on my meeting with him, I felt he would be a great fit for the team and the company.

When I told him he didn't pass the interview, he was really cool about it and asked if there was anything that I could do. I told him that I would speak to the vice president in charge of that project when I had the chance. And I told him he could check in with me in 3 weeks.

3 weeks passed and the vice president had been so busy I hadn't been able to speak to him yet. When the candidate e-mailed me back in exactly 3 weeks to follow up, I told him to check back with me in another 3 weeks. Of course by the time he followed up with me, I still hadn't had the chance to speak to the VP about him, so I told him to follow up within 2 weeks.

Right before that 2 week period was up, I tracked down the VP and spoke to him about this candidate, and the VP agreed to have some of his other team members interview him. I set up the interview, and low and behold he got the job!

What I was able to do for him is something I probably can't do for most people. What's more important here is that you are going to have to have some sort of respect and relationship with a recruiter for a recruiter to put themselves on the line like that.

If that candidate was rude to me, do you think I would have gone out of my way to help him like I did? If the candidate had bothered or pestered me too much, do you think I would have done what I did? The answer is no. If that had occurred, why would I do something that I don't have too? Why would I even consider questioning the person who interviewed him or the comments he made?

The fact is I really believed in this candidate, and looking back on it, his actions proved that I was right.

Following up with Recruiters

That brings up another important point. I think it's fair if you want to follow up with a recruiter about getting feedback on how an interview went or if the hiring manager wants to interview you, but you have to be careful you don't turn into a nuisance. That is the quickest way to lose favor with a recruiter. We have plenty of people e-mailing and calling us, and we want you to be respectful of our time just like we are of yours.

Not too long ago, I had a candidate call me 6 times within 2 hours before I was able to pick up his call. This was my response to him. "I saw that you called 6 times in the last 2 hours. What do you want?" He got pretty quiet and got off the phone very quickly. I think he realized I had no intention of wanting to deal with him again. If you are calling someone that much in that short period of time, what do you think a person is going to think about you? Hiring someone can sometimes be a long process, and if they are going to have to deal with you that much, it's simply not worth it. We have a lot of other candidates to deal with and positions to fill. Plus what are you going to be like once you are an employee?

What I recommend doing is asking the recruiter, "If I haven't heard back with you within a week, would that be a good time for me to follow up with you?" Or you could ask the recruiter, "When would be a good time for me to follow up with you?" Once the recruiter gives you an answer, then you should feel free to follow up at that time. The truth is at that time the recruiter may or may not have any more information for you, but you can always repeat that process until you get a definitive response. Respect for their time and good manners are helpful in building a good rapport with recruiters.

Don't forget that sometimes it's like pulling teeth to get an interview or to get any feedback on a resume we sent to a hiring manager. It's not uncommon for me to send a resume multiple times to a hiring manager over the course of a month before I finally get him to respond back to me.

Another interesting thing I have seen as a recruiter is that there seem to be a lot of people who feel very entitled and have a lot of demands and expectations that cost them the potential to interview or even the job.

Real-Life Example

I was working at a recruiting agency, and I came across a pretty good candidate whose salary expectations were around $140,000. But he only had 7 years of experience, and his resume wasn't as strong as it could be. Since I knew the client really well, I knew his resume wasn't going to entice them, especially with his unrealistic salary expectations attached to it. So I asked if he could strengthen his resume a bit, which probably would have taken no longer than 10 minutes. Not only did he refuse to update his resume, but he also became defensive with me regarding how he never had to go out of his way to get a job before and wasn't going to begin now.

I sent his resume to the client, as is, and of course they passed on him. But let's face the facts; if you can't spend an extra 10 or even 15 minutes to do something right and make a good first impression, what is that saying about your professionalism and the quality of work that you are going to produce? Being unwilling to update your resume and a poor attitude also scares recruiters away because if we had the chance to promote your skills to potential employers, we aren't likely to do that now; it is not just because of rudeness, but because you have now become a liability to us because we aren't sure how easy or hard it is going to be to deal with you moving forward. So we would rather just move on and forget about you.

Important Tip

I've given you several examples of why a recruiter might not submit your resume to hiring managers even if you seem like the perfect candidate; however, even if you do everything else right, there is 1 other reason they might not submit your resume to a hiring manager.

A recruiter's job is to fill a position. If they already have enough candidates in place and they think that one of those candidates can fill that position, why should they submit your resume? This only means more work for them.

Real-Life Example

This actually happened to me once; I was applying for a recruiting job at a great company. I phone interviewed with the recruiter who told me that they just sent a candidate in for a 2nd interview, and they wanted to wait to see how that interview worked out before they interviewed another person. They thought he was going to get the job.

I must admit that I was floored. I thought to myself, I'm better than that person. Let me have the job! Of course it doesn't work that way. My resume was never sent over to the hiring manager. I was kept out of a job that I was a great fit for because the recruiter didn't want to ruin what she already had going.

Things like that happen from time to time, and it's frustrating when you are the candidate. ... I know.

At the end of the day, we really want to believe everyone and trust everyone, and I'd like to think that most of the time you can. But you never really do know if what a recruiter is saying is true.

For example, they might know something that they aren't allowed to tell you. Or they might even tell you something as harmless as, "The hiring manager doesn't think you are a fit for anything we have right now, but we will keep you in mind in case something else opens up." Chances are that may not be the case. It does happen; don't get me wrong, but no one wants to tell someone that they weren't good enough to get the job. Those conversations usually don't go over too well.

Lastly, the best reason to have a good relationship with a recruiter is you never know when they are going to help you. I have given some examples, but anything can happen at any time. By having a good relationship with them—especially if you can be on the phone with them instead of trading e-mails—you never know what they may tell you. For example, they might tell you what it is like at the company, what you should do to prepare for an interview, what the hiring manager is like, or what you might actually be able to get as a salary! So treat them well; they might be your biggest ally to getting your dream job!

Chapter 11

USE INGENUITY TO GET YOUR FOOT IN THE DOOR

You've figured out which company or companies where you would like to work; you've tailored your resume to match the job descriptions; and you've applied for the job or jobs you want. What do you do if no one calls you back?

As I've mentioned throughout this book, lack of response to your job application doesn't mean you aren't a fit for a particular position or a particular company. It might just mean that no one has noticed your resume. Or it could mean that the people doing the hiring are simply unclear about what you bring to the table.

To get an interview, you may need to come up with a creative strategy for showcasing your skills to the people doing the hiring. You might need to use some ingenuity to get your foot in the door.

Real-Life Example

During the "Occupy Wall Street" movement, passersby's often yelled at the protesters to go out and get a job. One enterprising woman actually heeded that advice. She made a sign that said she was looking for work, and she started handing her resumes out to people who were walking by. A hiring manager for a Wall Street firm collected one of those resumes and wound up hiring this protester. It turned out she had a background that was of value to his company.

I applaud this protester's creativity. Fortunately, however, you don't have to join a protest movement to get an interview. There are other techniques that are much less difficult and time-consuming. I will provide more details on some techniques in this chapter.

Identifying Your Targets

The first step is to identify the company or companies you want to work for, along with the names of the managers who hire people with your background. Research the names of the directors or executives of these companies. Make a list of these names, e-mail addresses, and phone numbers. This is the kind of research that professional sales people conduct all the time. In case you didn't know, you are a professional salesperson because you are selling yourself!

Often you can get contact and other information from a company's website. If it's a smaller company, then the executives at the company are going to be much more involved in the hiring process. Get their names also.

LinkedIn can be another source for this information. Search by company, by title, and by other relevant filters. On the lower right side of each profile, you will see a section called "viewers of this profile also viewed..." It will contain a list of profiles you can click on. Many times these people have similar roles at the same company, which can help point you to other potential contacts.

Sometimes people on LinkedIn list their names as "private," which means that you can only see the word "private" where their name would normally be listed or you may only be able to see their first name. To get around this, go to the section of the profile page that says, "Viewers of this profile also viewed…" Click on these names, go to the same section of their profiles, and you may be able to see the full name of the person who had wanted to remain private. I have no clue why this loophole exists, but you might as well take advantage of it while it does.

Once you have the names of the people you want to contact, a little internet research will often turn up their direct e-mail addresses. One good source is Data.com, which was called Jigsaw.com before it was acquired by Salesforce.com. Another pretty good source for e-mail addresses is Lead411.com.

Another way to get an e-mail address is to simply call the company and see if anyone will give it to you. If that doesn't work, you can try to figure out your contact's e-mail address based on the structure of other addresses in the company. For example, if you're trying to reach Bruce Smith and another person's email at the same company is firstname.lastname@XYZCompany.com, try bruce.smith@XYZCompany.com. However, sometimes people who work at the same company have different e-mail structures, so you might want to try to verify a person's e-mail address before you send a random email.

Reaching Out to Potential Contacts

Now that you have the contact information for the hiring managers and other key people in your job search, how do you reach out to them? My favorite technique is to mail an actual letter. Fewer people do this these days, so your resume will stand out from the rest. One of my clients mailed his resume to a hiring manager at another company, and he actually got an e-mail back the very next day. The impressed hiring manager said, "What's old is new again." My client got the interview and the job!

Another approach is to send an e-mail, either through your standard e-mail account or through a social media account such as LinkedIn, Facebook, or Twitter. I recommend using your personal e-mail account because you can craft the subject of the e-mail to fit your circumstances, and you can attach your resume. The downside is that hiring managers sometimes get more than one hundred e-mails a day, and yours may get little or no attention. Your chances improve if your background exactly matches the hiring manager's needs.

Another way to increase your probability of success with this method is to send an e-mail to more than one hiring manager. When you copy multiple people at a company, there's a greater chance that the recipients will think it's important. To further increase your effectiveness, consider leaving the intended recipients a voicemail after their office hours to introduce yourself and to let them know that you are going to be following up with an e-mail. That way you have a better chance that they are going to be on the lookout for your e-mail and get back to you.

Calling the day after you send the e-mail is also a good idea. Mention in your e-mail that you will be following up with a phone call so that they will be expecting to hear from you. That might also increase your chances of them responding back to your e-mail after you send it.

Instead of asking for a job, consider asking for advice. Most people love to give advice; it makes them feel good. This approach also removes some of the pressure because you aren't putting the hiring manager on the spot to make a decision. If you are able to develop some sort of relationship, either on the phone or in person, that person might be more willing to help you or even go the extra mile. As I mentioned, I have done that for certain candidates who cultivated a relationship with me.

Do your homework. Know what you want to say and what questions you want to ask, so you don't waste people's time. Make the best use of every opportunity by efficiently and clearly explaining what you can offer. Update your resume and answer the interview preparation questions that I wrote about earlier, so that you can talk about your accomplishments at the drop of a hat.

Ingenuity Gets the Interview: A Real-Life Example

Years ago there was a growing company located in Silicon Valley that I really wanted to work for; however, I had several strikes against me. First, I was living on the other side of the country. Second, from viewing LinkedIn I could see that many of the recruiters working there had previously worked at companies like Google and Apple, and I had no experience with the type of companies found in Silicon Valley. Third, there were, no doubt, plenty of qualified candidates who lived within an easy commute of that company's offices.

With these odds against me, I knew that applying online was unlikely to work. I had to come up with a way to differentiate myself from everyone else. So I decided to be more creative.

Although I had chalked up some tremendous accomplishments at my company, I felt my resume did not give a clear picture of who I was, what I had accomplished, how significant some of my accomplishments really were, or what I could accomplish. So, I wrote a passionate cover letter about some of my capabilities and accomplishments. Next, I put together a success story about how I was a critical part of a huge staffing project. It described what we learned as a team and what contributed to our success, as well as our end results. Then, I sent the package via Federal Express to the company's VP of human resources.

Two months went by without a word. Then one of their recruiters contacted me. He mentioned that many people were impressed with my approach, and he arranged for me to have a phone interview with the director of recruiting. By that time I had already made other plans, so nothing came of it, except that I gained some great experience.

Consider for a minute how much more powerful and effective my approach was than merely applying online or even sending an e-mail to the VP with my resume and a cover letter. It allowed me to provide a comprehensive picture of my capabilities and goals. Plus, I gave the people doing the hiring a tangible package they could hold in their hands. Very few candidates are making this sort of effort, and it made me really stand out.

Better Next Time

This strategy worked extremely well, but next time I would do a few things differently. For instance, I would find out the name of the director of recruiting and send my package to him, since he probably would have the final say about who gets hired within the recruiting department. Or better yet, maybe I would send my resume package to the director of recruiting *and* the VP of human resources. That might have elicited an even greater response.

Another thing I would do differently is to put together a "brag book" and send it with my resume package. Nicely formatted on high-quality paper, it would contain all the "kudos" that co-workers and bosses had sent me. I'll go over this in greater detail in the next chapter, but if I was sending it out in a letter, here's how it might look:

I'm a recruiter for a multibillion dollar publicly traded company. Here's what the leadership team says about my performance.

> **From the CEO:** "You did an incredible job."
> **From the COO:** "Thanks for that big effort you gave; that was a challenging project and an important one to the company."

Continuing down the paper, I would have listed everyone's comments, from the senior vice president of Human Resources, the other vice presidents, and my boss. I believe this would have generated strong interest.

I also would have sent a case study instead of the success story. A case study would have allowed me to go into more depth about the challenges we faced, how I overcame them, and the results we achieved. Alternatively, I could have put together a business plan describing what I would do if I were hired.

When you go to great lengths to show recruiters and hiring managers your accomplishments and your capabilities, they will sit up and take notice. They will appreciate your initiative and will be more inclined to interview you. When you put forth this type of extra effort, you'll have a much better chance of getting your foot in the door. Your resume will stand out from the online applications, most of which at best get a thirty-second glance.

In addition to mailing your information, another good technique is to pick up the phone and give the hiring manager a call. This was commonly done before the advent of the internet, and it still works today. One of my friends got his job this way. He said to the hiring manager, "Wouldn't you rather have someone who showed enough initiative to call?" Before making the call, prepare and practice your "thirty-second elevator pitch," so you can present your qualifications quickly and convincingly.

Advertise

Companies advertise their products and services all the time, so why can't you? That's right. One effective way to get a job is to advertise yourself!

Companies like Facebook, LinkedIn, and Twitter all sell advertisements through their websites. With their pay-per-click format, you only have to pay money when someone clicks on your advertisement. What's more, you can target your advertisement to your specific market.

For example, on Facebook you can target your ad by age, gender, and interests; most importantly, you can even target your ad to the specific company that employs the person you want to reach.

For example, if you want to work at Apple, you can structure an ad so that only people who list Apple as their workplace can view it. You even can address it to "Apple employees," so when they see it, they will be more inclined to click on it.

Before I decided to FedEx my letter to the company I wanted to work for, I was thinking about using this tactic. I was going to take out an ad on Facebook and target it to the company and have it say something like, "Hey 'Company X' employees, I'm a pretty good recruiter and I'd like to work for you." (Actually, my original text was a bit cleverer and it rhymed, but you get the idea.) Once someone clicked on the ad, it would have sent them to my LinkedIn account, where my full resume and accompanying recommendations would be posted.

This approach would have also demonstrated my willingness to do what it took to get the job, and I believe management would also have been impressed with the creativity and initiative I exercised. You can do similar things on LinkedIn and Twitter, but I prefer Facebook because it's more popular. People even use it at work, unless their company has blocked access.

Google Ads

A few years ago, I recall hearing a story about how someone advertised himself on Google. He bought the key words that matched the names of the hiring managers he wanted to work for, so that when those hiring managers Googled themselves, they would be directed to this candidate's ad. The ad was actually a note that encouraged the reader to call the candidate to discuss possible employment. The idea worked! All of these managers reached out to him, and he eventually landed the position he wanted.

The candidate only spent around $5.00 on this pay-per-click marketing campaign. Of course, if he had tried to get the attention of Bill Gates or Mark Zuckerberg, he could have spent considerably more because lots of people Google those names. If you use this approach, keep in mind that you never know who is going to be searching for that hiring manager's name and come across the note that you wrote.

Persistence

In this chapter, I've told you about several creative strategies for getting your foot in the door. I'm sure you can think of plenty more. However, if you are proactively conducting your search and continually building your network, you may not need to take these steps.

Persistence is the key to success. I hired one candidate who had applied to 56 different positions during the previous twelve months. I know another person who persevered for four years before he finally landed the job of his dreams. These people eventually succeeded because they didn't give up.

If one idea doesn't work, try another and another and another, until one eventually pays off. If you persevere, then you will eventually get your foot in the right door!

Chapter 12

INTERVIEW
IMPRESSIVELY

As a recruiter, whenever I ask candidates how they thought their interview went, they almost always say "great." More often than not, however, I later have to inform them that they didn't get the job. Many can't seem to understand why. Some even become argumentative.

It's taken me ten years to figure it out, but I finally understand why these candidates were unsuccessful. All of them made the same mistake. They didn't convince the interviewer they were right for the job. As I have said, hiring is risk management. It's easier for a hiring manager to say no to a candidate than to say yes.

The Successful Interview

To be successful in an interview, you must

- Thoroughly understand the company and the position for which you are applying

91

- Understand how your background and capabilities will enable you to be successful in this position
- Understand the hiring manager's expectations
- Convince the hiring manager that you will meet or surpass those expectations.

If you are able to accomplish all of these things, you have a good chance of besting other candidates for the position, even if you're not the most qualified in terms of education and experience.

Real-Life Illustration

Here are some actual notes that a hiring manager made regarding three candidates he had interviewed for a high-level job. I've made some observations about what each candidate did well and not so well.

- **Candidate #1**

"He has a good understanding of the challenges we are facing and a pretty good idea about how we can fix them. My only issue is that he envisioned rolling out his solutions at a much slower pace than what we would like."

Observation: This candidate was well qualified for the position, but he apparently never bothered to ask about the hiring manager's expectations. If he had, he might have sensed the urgency of the situation and responded accordingly.

- **Candidate #2**

"He has a really good background of experience in the areas that are important to us, and he understands the pros and cons of our current business organization and operation. However, he was unable to express how he would solve our problems. He spoke mostly about his past accomplishments and said little about how he would accomplish our goals."

Observation: This candidate also seemed to be well qualified for the position, but he failed to demonstrate to the hiring manager how would accomplish the company's goals.

- **Candidate #3**

"This candidate was very well prepared. While he isn't the strongest candidate from a knowledge standpoint, he understands our needs, and he related his past accomplishments to the work he would be doing. I was impressed that he had prepared a Power Point presentation with specific timelines to show how he would tackle the problems and what he would do in order to achieve our goals."

Observation: Even though this candidate was possibly the least knowledgeable (he was certainly the least senior because the other two were already vice presidents), he obviously had prepared well for the interview. He knew what the expectations were for this position, and he had developed a plan to meet them. Not surprisingly, this candidate got the job!

Time spent preparing for an interview pays big dividends. This candidate was promoted to vice president and given a $35,000 per year pay increase, with the opportunity to earn another 30 percent in bonuses. That's a pretty nice return on investment!

Prepare for Success

You can have the same type of success in your interviews if you take the time to prepare. The key is to know in advance what you want to say about your background and skills. It's not helpful to say that you are a hardworking and self-motivated individual. Most people already assume that. Give specifics about what you have accomplished.

For example, if I were being interviewed for a position in recruiting, I might tell how once, when I had only seven days to staff a new project, I worked twelve hours a day and filled all of the open positions in only four days, which saved the company $50,000.

When you are prepared, you will be able to answer just about any question the interviewer throws at you. Even if you don't know the exact answer, you'll be in control of the situation, so you can talk about what you do know. Of course, if you don't know the answer to a specific question, say so.

Over the years, I've noticed on post interview assessments that hiring managers highly value integrity. If you are honest and say you don't know the answer to a question, it's possible you won't get the job. But if you try to BS your way through an interview, then you almost certainly won't get the job.

Explaining Your Process

In addition to talking about what you have accomplished, you need to be able to clearly explain how you accomplished it. Convince the interviewer that your success is not just chance, but rather the result of a deliberate process.

For example, if you were interviewing for a position in sales, and the interviewer asked about your performance, you might say something like this:

> "I have been in sales for more than eight years, and I exceeded my quota by more than 20 percent each year. I was able to do this by making fifty cold calls a day and setting up five meetings per week. As a result of some training I received from the previous vice president of sales, I learned to do my research ahead of time. I knew who I was going to call on, what I was going to say, and what results I wanted. I also found it helpful to make my cold calls in the morning, when I would not be interrupted. Then I would focus on sales meetings during the rest of the day."

Obviously, this answer is much more convincing than a simple reply without elaboration about the process. When you give a complete answer, you come across as confident and competent. When you explain the process that contributed to your success, you are much more believable, and people are more likely to hire you. Other candidates might have significant achievements to their credit, but if they don't explain how they achieved their accomplishments, then you will have a better chance at winning the job.

This technique works for any position. For example, if you are an executive assistant and you are interviewing for a new position, you might say something like this:

> "In my past position as the executive assistant for the CEO and members of his executive staff, I handled more than 100 telephone calls a day and scheduled more than twenty-five appointments a week. In addition, I took care of all travel arrangements. Every morning I would meet with the CEO for ten minutes to go over what he wanted to accomplish that day and to see if there were any items that needed immediate attention. At the end of the day, we'd meet again to make sure we had accomplished everything on our to-do list. Then we'd go over the agenda for the next day."

Interview Preparation Questions

Prepare for your interview by answering the following questions:

1. **Why do I want to work at this company?**
   You will probably be asked this question, so take time to write out a one-paragraph answer about why you would be excited to work for this company.

2. **What does this company do?**
   Write a paragraph about the company's products or services. Is the company profitable? How does it make its money?

3. **What is the company like?**
   What do you know about the company's culture? Have you discovered anything online or elsewhere that concerns you? Think ahead about how you will bring up these concerns in an appropriate manner.

4. **What value would I bring to this company?**

   How do your skills match the company's needs? Write down specific examples and be prepared to speak about them.

5. **What ten questions about the company would I like to ask?**

   Some interviewers will interpret a lack of questions as a lack of interest. Be prepared to ask at least ten questions, even if you think you know the answers to some of them. It's important to have at least ten in mind because some of them will almost certainly be answered in the course of your interview, so you won't get to use them.

6. **What will you talk about if you need to engage in small talk?**

   Think of some possible light topics to discuss to break the ice. Having some topics in mind will help you feel more at ease during lulls in the conversation, such as when you are being escorted to a conference room or are waiting for a meeting to start.

Questions to Expect

In your interview, you can almost certainly expect to be asked the following questions, so do your homework:

1. **Tell me about yourself.**

   This is a very common question, so be prepared. Don't bore the interviewer. Stick to the essential and relevant facts, and make them interesting. No one wants to know about how you were picked on in elementary school because you were overweight. Use this opportunity to explain how you got into your current career and industry. Mention some of your biggest accomplishments, and tell how you contributed to the efforts of your team.

2. **What are your most significant accomplishments?**

   Give specific numbers and tell how your accomplishments benefited the company. For example if you worked in marketing for a product development company, you might say something like the following:

"We had a good product, but I didn't think our sales were as high as they should be. So I put together a focus group that pinpointed another target market. I then led the development of a marketing campaign to re-launch the product. This resulted in an additional $10 million dollars in annual revenues."

3. **What were your biggest disappointments? What mistakes did you learn the most from?**

   Think ahead of time about how you will answer this question. You need to be honest, but you don't want to appear incompetent.

4. **Tell me about a time you worked as part of a team?**

   Have a couple of examples in mind.

5. **Why do you want to work for this company?**

   Let your enthusiasm show!

Your Pre-interview Plan

After you have answered all the above questions, develop a preliminary plan describing how you will tackle the challenges of the position for which you are applying. I call it a preliminary plan because you will no doubt need to adjust it as you glean more information during the course of the interview. Your idea of what the position will entail might turn out to be quite different after you learn what the hiring manager actually thinks and expects. However, when you plan ahead, you will be more in control even when things change.

- **How will your past success help you succeed in this position?**

  Write down specific examples.

- **What do you envision yourself doing in this job?**

  Consider preparing a PowerPoint presentation or other documents outlining your approach. Even if you don't get to use them in the interview, they will help you more intelligently answer questions.

Your Brag Book

There is one other important thing you should take to your interview in addition to your resume. It's called your "brag book." It will consist of the kudos you have received from your superiors and co-workers. These might be in the form of e-mails, letters, awards, or personal notes.

If you are asked in the interview what other people think of your performance, simply pull out this brag book and let these documents speak for themselves. Or if you prefer, you can bring up these points orally during the interview. Because you have prepared the brag book in advance, you will know exactly what you want to say.

In your brag book, you can also include copies of your white papers, case studies, plans, or other reports and projects. For each item, point out how your efforts positively benefited the company and make sure you quantify those results.

The 90-Day Preliminary Business Plan

The interview is really a sales presentation. Now that you have done your homework, your job is to convince the interviewer that you understand the requirements of the job and are the best person to accomplish them. To do that, I suggest that you develop a "ninety-day preliminary business plan" while you are being interviewed. Its purpose is to state how you would address the position's most urgent issues during your first ninety days on the job.

Before you can develop this plan, you need to thoroughly understand the company's needs. After you have established rapport in the interview, ask the following questions:

1. What are you looking for in a candidate, and what do they have to do in order to be successful?
2. Why is this position open?
3. What do you hope to accomplish by filling this position?
4. What are the major goals/initiatives you would like to see accomplished?

5. How soon would you like these done?
6. Who are the stakeholders (other people or groups I would be working with)?
7. What are some other daily responsibilities?

As your questions are being answered, I suggest that you write out key goals on a whiteboard. If this doesn't suit your personality, or if a whiteboard isn't available, you can simply write the answers you are given on a sheet of paper. Ask about priorities, and separate the goals into three categories: thirty days, sixty days, and ninety days.

Next, lay out your plan for accomplishing these goals within the prescribed time frames. You won't be expected to know everything, so, when necessary, ask questions to get more information. Once you have laid out your plan, ask if there any questions. Close by saying something like, "Does this describe what you would like me to come in and do?"

Within twenty-four hours after the interview, send a follow-up letter (an e-mail is also acceptable, although not quite as good in my opinion), expressing your appreciation for the interview and summarizing your preliminary ninety-day business plan. Let the hiring manager know that you welcome feedback and that you are willing to talk over your plan and any other questions that arise.

You can use any number of formats for your plan. Here is a simple one to give you an idea:

- Within the first two weeks, I will meet with all the stakeholders.
- Within thirty days, I will do _____.
- After thirty days, I will meet with management to discuss our progress and get feedback about what adjustments need to be made.
- Within sixty days, I will _____

Your actual plan will include more detail, but it doesn't need to be lengthy. The point is to illustrate your understanding of the problems and your ability to implement solutions. This approach will put you miles ahead of everyone else who is interviewing for this position.

A Real-Life Example

Here's the true story about how this interviewing technique evolved. Once when I was interviewing for a job that I really wanted, I decided to build a business plan that described what I would do to increase the company's revenues. During my interview, I went over my plan with the hiring manager, and he seemed impressed.

A week went by, and I didn't hear from the hiring manager. So I called the company and found out that someone else had taken his place. A few days later, I was called back in to meet with the new manager.

During the interview, the new hiring manager told me that she had thrown out all of the resumes that the old manager was considering, but that the corner of a blue folder in her trashcan had caught her eye. When she picked it up, it happened to be my business plan. She said she was very impressed with it and showed it to her boss. That's why she called me in for an interview!

After we chatted a bit, she put me on the phone with the vice president, who was working out of another location. He told me that he liked my business plan. As soon as I got off the phone with the vice president, I was offered the job!

Few candidates go to the trouble to learn about what a company does, how it makes money, and what its problems are. Most don't spend time thinking about how they can make a positive impact. When you do these things, you will come across in the interview as alert, knowledgeable, and motivated. Hiring managers will view you as an asset, not a risk. When you know exactly what you are getting into and what is expected of you, you will be able to hit the ground running.

Chapter 13

NEGOTIATE FROM STRENGTH

The best negotiations are win-win situations or at least they are perceived that way by both parties. If you fight so hard to get what you want that the other party feels cheated, then you will ultimately lose. At the same time, if you fail to negotiate aggressively to achieve what you deserve and desire, then you will ultimately lose. A good negotiation satisfies both sides.

To achieve your objectives in negotiation, you must negotiate from strength. You must know what you want and be willing to walk away if you don't get it. On the other hand, if you try to bluff, the other party may call your bluff and walk away from the deal.

To negotiate from strength, do the following:

1. **Ask for more money.**

   Most candidates I deal with never ask for more money or other benefits, and it's not uncommon for them to accept a position for $10,000 or $15,000 less than what the company could pay.

2. **Know what you are worth.**
   We covered this important point in chapter 5.

3. **Convince the hiring manager that you will be an asset, not a risk.**
   We talked about this in chapter 12.

4. **Get two offers in hand before making a decision about which one to accept.**
   You can accomplish this more easily if you have your network in place, as we discussed in chapter 8.

5. **If possible, remain in your current job while you are interviewing.**
   When you are employed, you will feel less pressure to accept the first offer that comes along.

6. **Assess the hiring manager's urgency.**
   You will have more leverage if you know how urgently the company needs to fill the position.

The above factors are listed in approximate order of importance. For example, even if you don't have two offers in hand, you can still be in a strong negotiating position if you know what you are worth. And even if the hiring manager is not under excessive pressure to fill the position, you are in a strong negotiating position if you are able to convince the hiring manager that you are an asset, not a risk. Most importantly, to get more money, you must ask for it. No one is just going to give you an offer and then voluntarily give you additional money without your asking.

Negotiating Salary

When evaluating job offers, salary and benefits are only two of many factors to be considered. In some cases, they might not even be the most important. However, for most job candidates, they rank right up near the top, so you should know how to negotiate to get the salary and benefits you merit.

Most people are poor negotiators. They are so relieved to get a job offer that they accept the first one without asking for more money. Others are simply too timid to bargain.

The best time to negotiate for more compensation is after you have been offered the job. At that point, it is highly unlikely that the company will rescind the offer. If you know what you're worth and you have made a persuasive case that you will be an asset, you are in a strong position to ask for more. You can walk away if you do not get what you think you deserve.

Keep in mind that the company may not be able to give you an immediate answer. The hiring manager may need to consult with other people to get approval or management may need to move some money from one budget to another.

With that being said, these days' recruiters may obtain your salary and benefits expectations up front and present that information to the hiring manager. They might work with you to agree to a certain level of compensation before you even go into an interview. The plus to that is that you know what you are walking into and you can avoid wasting your time. Of course, if you have done all your research ahead of time, you should already have a good idea of what compensation you can expect.

The down side of negotiating your salary with the recruiter up front is that if you ask for too much, then you might price yourself out of consideration before you even go in for an interview. Your goal should be to get into the interview, so you can prove to the manager what an incredible candidate you are. Then you will have a greater chance in getting the compensation you desire.

Use Caution When Giving Salary Ranges

If you do have to give your salary expectations upfront, I usually recommend giving a number rather than a salary range because that leaves your desired salary to be determined by someone other than you. For example, let's say you tell a recruiter or a hiring manager that you are looking for a salary between $110,000 - $120,000 many times the hiring manager will interpret your actual salary request and what it will take to bring you on as $110,000. Where as in your head you may really be looking for $120,000.

Then if they offer you $110,000 now you have limited how much you can negotiate for because they know the exact range you want. In addition, if you ask for more than $120,000 at this point, they are going to wonder why you are changing your salary request on them at the last minute. I have seen a good deal of candidates get the short end of the stick by beginning negotiating with a salary range.

You are much better off figuring out what you are worth and trying to figure out what the company can pay and then letting them know what you are looking for salary wise. Usually you are better off asking for a salary that is on the higher end, so you can negotiate down if you have to.

A Recruiter's Role in Salary Negotiations

In my experience as a recruiter, I learned that most companies have three different salary levels for new hires:

1. **Target salary**: the starting salary the company would like to pay.

2. **Stated maximum salary**: the maximum salary the company's management says it is willing to pay. This is the maximum figure given to recruiters. Many times, the stated maximum salary might function as the target salary.

3. **Actual maximum salary**: the maximum salary the company is *actually* willing to pay. Most hiring managers never mention this figure to the recruiter until they have to during the course of a negotiation.

Three Real-Life Experiences

When I was a young recruiter at a recruiting agency, a hiring manager complained that I had not been sending him enough candidates. "I can't find any within the pay range you've specified," I told him. In a raised voice he said, "Send them to me anyway. You're a recruiter. You should know that I can pay more than what I've told you!" I have since learned that companies can almost always pay more than what they have originally told the recruiter.

On another occasion, I was working to fill a position with a target salary of $125,000. I couldn't find any candidates within that salary range, and the hiring manager was becoming increasingly frustrated. In desperation, I sent over a good candidate, but I wasn't optimistic because she wanted $140,000.

The hiring manager interviewed her and made an offer for $143,000, plus a bonus to pay for a hotel room during relocation. This was a shock to me. I had been working with this hiring manager for some time to recruit other candidates for the same position, and she had never given any indication she would go above $125,000.

Why was this candidate able to negotiate for almost $20,000 more than the company originally intended to pay? The reason was because she was negotiating from strength. She had the following five factors in her favor:

1. She sensed that the company desperately needed to fill this position.

2. She was aware that she had proven to the hiring manager that she was a valuable asset.

3. She had an idea of what she could get elsewhere.

4. She was willing to walk away if the company couldn't meet her salary expectations.

5. She asked for the money.

At another time I was working to fill a position with a target salary of $90,000 and a maximum salary of $98,000. The hiring manager told me in no uncertain terms not to send him candidates who wanted more than the maximum salary. The very next day, this hiring manager sent me the resume of a candidate he wanted to hire. I was floored to see that he mentioned he could pay a salary of $110,000 for this candidate. Apparently this candidate had specific skills that the hiring manager considered extremely valuable. Was this candidate really worth the extra money? Possibly, but candidates who do great in an interview and are able to successfully negotiate a very high salary can also fail in their job just like everyone else.

These are examples of how companies will stretch their salary parameters when candidates negotiate from strength. Many times management can pay more money than the stated maximum for a position.

Downward Pressures

I don't want to give the impression that companies are always able and willing to pay more than the specified starting salary for a position. Sometimes a hiring manager will want to pay more, but a group vice president will either veto that decision or ask for justification. Most of the time, however, hiring managers are able to justify and get what they want.

Some hiring managers put downward pressure on salaries, even when they don't absolutely need to. For instance, if they find out what a candidate's current salary is, they might offer only $5,000 to $10,000 more, even if the position is structured to pay $20,000 or $30,000 more.

Some hiring managers are concerned about what is called internal equity. That is, they consider it unfair to hire new employees at salaries that are higher than the salaries they pay their current employees who are performing well in equivalent positions. I mention this because you could run into this type of ceiling during your salary negotiations. You will not be aware of it because they aren't going to tell you.

If you are not able to break through this ceiling during negotiations, you might have to be prepared to walk away. I have noticed that companies who benchmark candidates in this way usually compare them to their most outstanding performers, many of whom could be getting a lot more money elsewhere. Perhaps that is why these hiring managers are so sensitive about bringing in employees who are making more than their top employees.

Another Real-Life Experience

Once when I was seeking to staff a help-desk team, we had to fill five positions quickly. The target salary was $45,000, and the maximum listed salary was $50,000. We eventually narrowed the search down to the following five candidates:

	Current Salary	Desired Salary
Candidate 1	$42,000	$42,000 or more
Candidate 2	$36,000	$40,000
Candidate 3	$42,000	$42,000 or more
Candidate 4	$35,000	$40,000
Candidate 5	$60,000	$60,000

Here are some interesting facts about the negotiations with these candidates:

- None had other job interviews lined up.

- None had done any research, so they really didn't have a clue what they were worth.

- Four out of five asked for less money than the maximum specified for the job.

- None was alert enough to realize that the company urgently needed to fill these positions, so they forfeited this potential negotiating weapon.

Here are the offers that were made to these candidates, along with the reasons for the salary differentials:

	Salary Offered	Reason Why
Candidate 1	$44,000	Multiple certifications
Candidate 2	$40,000	Multiple certifications
Candidate 3	$42,500	Only one year of experience
Candidate 4	$35,500	Less than one year of experience
Candidate 5	$60,000	The most experience on the team

This hiring manager was so busy she spent only a few minutes structuring these job offers on her blackberry. She used what limited information she had on hand; thus, I don't think a lot of thought went into these job offers. Here are a few interesting observations:

- Education was given considerable weight, which is something that will vary from hiring manager to hiring manager.

- Experience was also given considerable weight.

- The hiring manager primarily used past salaries to determine the new starting salaries.

- The first four candidates almost certainly could have negotiated for higher salaries if they had used the techniques described in this chapter.

Tip

To assess how much power you have in the negotiation, casually ask the following questions during your interview:

- How long has this position been open?

- Why is it open (growth, turnover)?

- How soon do you need to fill this position?

If the hiring manager urgently needs to fill a position, there's a better chance you can negotiate for more money. Unfilled jobs can be extremely costly. For example, if a project slips because of understaffing, the hiring manager responsible for the project might be subject to considerable pressure and criticism. A delay in an important deliverable in a project or to a client could put not only the manager but also his boss and the entire executive team in hot water and might end up costing the company an enormous amount of revenue. In these types of pressure situations, I have seen hiring managers bend over backwards to get the candidate they want on board. Sometimes I have seen candidates ask for and receive more than even I thought was possible.

In my experience, the current salary and the salary expectations of most candidates are below the maximum salary companies are willing to pay. If you do your homework and use the negotiating techniques outlined in this chapter, you should be able to increase your starting pay significantly. It might not happen with the first company you interview, or even the second or third, but if you are negotiating from a position of strength, you'll eventually achieve the compensation you desire and deserve.

When negotiating a salary, take care that you don't appear to be playing games or pitting one company against another. It's perfectly acceptable to go back to a company who has made you an offer and ask for more money, especially if you have a legitimate counter offer from another company. However, don't try this more than once. At some point overly aggressive bargaining will cross an invisible line and be perceived as a slap in the face.

When you do need to reopen the salary negotiations, you might say something like this:

> "I am so excited to get this offer from you, and I am passionate about working for you and your company. However, I just received an offer from Company X that pays $5,000 more. Is there anything you can do?"

Real-Life Example

While working as a recruiter with a large company, a candidate I referred to a hiring manager was offered a job with a salary of $130,000 per year. As soon as the candidate received the offer, he e-mailed me saying that he had been offered another job with an annual salary of $147,000. The hiring manager authorized me to increase our offer to $145,000, which the candidate accepted.

Did the candidate have another job offer? Who knows, but he got a $15,000 bump in his salary simply by stating he had did. Just think about how important that extra money was going to be to him. It could have taken him two or three years of raises to bump up his annual salary by that amount. Because he started out at the higher salary, all of his future raises likely will be based on percentages of that higher amount.

Notice that it only took this candidate a few seconds to type out a one-sentence e-mail to me to ask for more money. Within a few minutes, the hiring manager responded, authorizing me to amend his offer for an extra $15,000. This candidate was able to bump up the offer for three reasons:

1. He knew what he was worth, as evidenced by the additional job offer.

2. He had the confidence to ask for more money.

3. He must have convinced the hiring manager that he would be an asset, not a risk because the hiring manager maintained interest. The manager realized that he really needed him in order to successfully complete his project, and he was willing to pay for it.

Never hesitate to ask for more money if you meet the above three conditions. If you don't ask for it, someone else will, and you could be the one who loses out. After all, where do you think companies get those $5 million-dollar signing bonuses they give to their CEOs? I'm sure they are asking for more money, and so should you!

Room to Maneuver

Companies may have quite a bit of flexibility in salary negotiations, so be sure to ask for what you think you are worth. Even if the salary for a particular position is budgeted for a certain amount, management can sometimes shift money from other budgets when that is necessary to attract a highly valued candidate. In fact, I suspect that this candidate could have negotiated for even more money if he really wanted to.

With that being said, even if a company has the ability to pay you more money, it may not want to for various reasons. For instance, management may have issues with internal equity, as we have discussed. Or perhaps the hiring manager thinks you are asking for more than you are worth or for a bigger salary increase than you deserve. You will also experience resistance if your salary request threatens the level of profitability the group must maintain.

Besides negotiating for salary, there are many other perks and benefits that you might be able to receive if you just ask. Those can range from flex time, telecommuting, and continuing education reimbursements. Below are some of the more common ones that may vary from company to company. One thing is for sure; as you climb the company ladder, the benefits that you are usually able to receive and negotiate for start increasing dramatically and can expand beyond the list I have included below.

Vacation Time

It amazes me to see how few job candidates negotiate for additional vacation time. Vacation time is extremely important, especially if you have a family and want to do some traveling. It also can translate into hard cash.

Let's say you're offered a new job paying $100,000 a year that comes with just fifteen days of vacation. Let's further assume that you negotiate for an additional five days of vacation, bringing your total to twenty days per year. If you only use fifteen days of vacation annually and bank the additional five days, at the end of five years, then you would have accrued twenty-five days of unused vacation time. Those days will be worth almost $10,000 before taxes, once you cash them in. And by the way that amount could increase if you had any raises because when you are paid out on your leftover vacation days the amount paid is based on your current salary. That extra bonus is certainly worth a few minutes of negotiating time!

I worked at one company that would readily give candidates with a certain level of experience an extra five days of vacation. But the candidates had to ask for it. Most candidates never did, so those candidates never received that extra vacation time. With that being said, some companies might have rigid vacation policies with no flexibility for negotiation. You won't know until you ask.

In this company, even many of the managers had only fifteen days of vacation, simply because they had not asked for more. When they found out about this inequity and realized they could have easily negotiated for more vacation time, they became bitter. They were especially resentful whenever new job candidates asked for additional vacation time during their salary negotiations.

Some companies with extremely liberal benefits, such as high-tech firms in Silicon Valley, regularly grant twenty or twenty-one days of vacation and unlimited sick leave. That's such a generous package that there may be little point in trying to negotiate more. But still, it pays to do some research to see what else you can negotiate. In these companies, instead of negotiating for more vacation days, you might want to focus on getting stock options, which can be much more lucrative.

Sign-on Bonuses

Sign-on bonuses are generally more common in booming economies. However, if you are a highly qualified candidate who has proven to a manager that you will be an asset, you stand a chance of receiving one even in tough economic times. These bonuses also tend to be more common if you work in certain industries, such as finance, or if you are a high-level manager and a company wants to entice you to join their company.

Even if you don't fit into one of these categories, I've seen sign-on bonuses range from $2,500 to as high as $20,000, with an average around $5,000. Of course, if you are a senior-level candidate or if you're interviewing with a Wall Street firm, you might be offered much more. I've seen some CEOs offered sign-on bonuses as high as seven figures.

Also, a company might be more willing to pay you a sign-on bonus if you have a legitimate need. For example, if you are leaving another company you might need money to pay back a tuition reimbursement you have used before you were fully vested in that benefit. If you need to relocate and the company does not offer a relocation allowance, you might want to ask for a bonus to cover those costs. That might be possible because the money for a sign-on bonus might come from a different pool of money than where a relocation allowance might be allocated. Keep in mind that bonuses are taxable. Ask for enough to net the amount you need.

Real-Life Experience

I had a position to fill that required a very senior candidate with expertise in a specific area. The maximum salary for the job was $135,000. I found an outstanding candidate, but he wanted an annual salary of $150,000, twenty days of vacation, a sign-on bonus of $5,000, and reimbursement for some specialized training.

I didn't have the heart to tell him that I thought he was crazy. I had been handling the hiring for this group for more than a year. During that time they had never offered a salary higher than their stated maximum, and they had never granted a sign-on bonus. Nevertheless, I e-mailed his compensation request to the management team.

Later that day I was asked to come to a meeting with the hiring manager, the hiring manager's boss, and the vice president of the group. I was certain they were going to tell me to try to reason with this candidate. You can imagine my surprise when they told me they had made a decision to give this candidate everything he had asked for. It turns out that the company needed this person for a high-priority project that had the potential to generate an additional $500,000 in revenue.

This candidate was aware that the position had been open for a while, that the need was urgent, and that we had no other qualified candidates. He used all of this knowledge to negotiate from strength. Would he have accepted an offer for only $150,000, without any additional benefits? I don't know. Maybe, or perhaps, he would have walked away. The management team simply wasn't prepared to take that risk.

Year-End Bonuses

Year-end bonuses vary considerably by industry, profession, and level of responsibility. Many companies have none. Companies that do have them usually have policies stipulating who will actually qualify for a bonus and how these bonuses relate to certain goals. Sometimes these goals are tied to individual performance, and sometimes they might be tied to the performance of a group. Bonuses might also be given out on a quarterly basis.

Bonuses are more common at the managerial level and with Wall Street firms and in other specific industries. When they do exist, I've seen them range from 5 percent to 50 percent of annual salary and sometimes more in the case of very senior-level candidates. For general mid-level management positions, I have seen an average range around 20 to 25 percent.

Do your research ahead of time to determine if you might be eligible for a bonus, and then use that information as leverage to work out your best possible deal. Keep in mind that within some companies, these bonuses may be rather rigidly determined according to levels of responsibility. At other companies they are negotiable. Don't overlook this topic in your negotiations. I have seen candidates negotiate a much larger bonus than what was originally offered.

Stock Options

Companies, both private and public, may offer job candidates and employees up to two forms of stock options: restricted and unrestricted. These two types of stock options differ greatly. If you are unfamiliar with how they work, I recommend you speak to a professional, so you clearly understand them.

Some companies only grant stock options to members of their management team. Others, like the high-tech companies of Silicon Valley, disperse them to all employees. If you have stock options with a rapidly growing, profitable company, then you can become rich regardless of your level of seniority.

If you are interviewing with a company that grants stock options, be sure to try to negotiate for them. If you don't know if a company grants employee stock options, then try getting the information from Glassdoor.com or Thevault.com, or simply ask during the hiring process.

Commissions

Unless you are working in some aspect of sales, you probably won't need to be concerned with commissions. However, if they are part of your compensation package and if you are confident of your sales ability, you might be offered the choice to take less in salary in return for a higher commission percentage. If you are new to sales, I recommend sticking with the higher base salary until you have built up your business. If you become a "rainmaker" at your company, then you will probably have greater flexibility in restructuring your deal, even though you are already an employee. Also keep in mind that commission rates can be negotiated from time to time.

While there are other perks, benefits and forms of compensation that you may be able to negotiate, the ones we just went over are the most common. If you do your research ahead of time, then you should have a better idea on what else a company might be able to offer and whether it is negotiable.

When Negotiating—What Not to Do

I once worked with a candidate who was upset with the low salary he was offered. He told us that based on Monster.com's salary guide, he should be getting $10,000 more. He also said that he called his old manager at a company where he used to work two jobs ago to find out what he would be earning if he had stayed. That manager had apparently confirmed the $10,000 figure.

This is not how to negotiate! Companies don't care what a website says about salaries. This candidate should have used the techniques described in chapter 5 of this book to determine his worth. What does it matter that he could have been earning $10,000 more if he had stayed in his old job? If his old job was that good, then why did he leave?

This guy was in a weak bargaining position. He didn't have any other job offers in hand, and he looked more like a fool than an asset. On the other hand, we were in a strong position because we had several other candidates interested in this position. In the end, we refused to budge in the negotiations, and he accepted our original offer.

Too Pushy for His Own Good

I once interviewed an unemployed candidate for a position that paid $135,000. But this candidate wanted $150,000, because that's what he thought our company was paying a friend of his for the same type of work. His friend was earning $135,000, but for confidentiality reasons, I could only tell this candidate that $150,000 was too high. Nevertheless, this fellow went into the interview and asked for the higher amount. The hiring manager didn't appreciate his pushy attitude and said, "It sounds like he is shopping us around trying to get the highest salary." In the end the hiring manager recommended that we not hire him.

A few months later, we had another similar opening that paid $140,000 per year, so I contacted this candidate. It turned out that he had already taken another job. I strongly suspect the salary was considerably less than what we were offering because I could tell he was tempted by the offer when he said it sounded like an incredible salary. However, he said he just accepted a position with a company and he didn't want to sever his relationship with that company, since it had taken him so long to find a job. If he had been more patient and reasonable, then he might have been given an offer for the original position in which he interviewed.

Too Much of a Hurry

Be careful about walking away from an offer. You never know how things are going to change in a short period of time. We gave an offer to an outstanding candidate for a salary of $160,000 plus a $5,000 signing bonus. He turned us down because he said he had a much better offer. A few weeks later, he came back and said that things hadn't worked out at the other job, so he was still available.

During those two weeks, we had filled a different position on the same project. It was budgeted for $100,000 a year, but we had to pay $120,000 plus a $5,000 sign-on bonus to get the person we wanted. To stay within budget, we borrowed the excess $20,000 from the $160,000 we had budgeted for the position we discussed with the first candidate, and we used that position's sign-on bonus. When the first candidate came back to us, we could offer him only $140,000 and no sign-on bonus. Needless to say, he wasn't too happy, but there wasn't much any of us could do. He was forced to accept our offer which was $25,000 less in total compensation than the original offer.

Non-Negotiables

One candidate I was working with wanted us to waive the three-year vesting period for the company-sponsored 401K. Of course, we couldn't do that. Even if we could, we wouldn't want to do it anyway because the whole point of having a vesting period is to promote retention.

Timing

Timing can also be a factor when it comes to negotiating compensation because more funds might be available at the beginning of a fiscal year or quarter. I once moved two people to Europe within the first two weeks of the fiscal year. This cost about $40,000, which was just about all that the company had budgeted for relocation for the entire quarter. If any other manager hired another candidate in our group and that candidate needed relocation and asked for it, then we would not have been able to give it to them because the money was gone. Of course, if we absolutely had to help someone else with relocation or a signing bonus, then we probably could have found the money somewhere. Many times I've seen money magically appear when someone up high enough in the company demanded it.

The Value of Job Codes and Job Titles

You need to be aware that many companies, especially the larger ones, use some sort of job code system to identify levels of responsibility. For example, a job code for an entry-level recruiter might be "Recruiter 1," which could be abbreviated "Recruit 1." A senior recruiter might be "Recruit 4." Let's suppose you accept a job as a Recruit 2. If after you are hired you discover that other recruiters with less experience are classified as Recruit 3, then you're likely going to feel shortchanged and angry.

Real-Life Example

A friend of mine who works at a large publicly held company was about to be promoted from an Engineer 2 to an Engineer 3. He told me that when you go from a 2 to a 3, you actually get an 8 to 9 percent raise, instead of the standard yearly 3.5 percent. Imagine if he had come on board as an Engineer 1 instead of an Engineer 2. He would then first have had to move up to Engineer 2 and stay in that job code for some time before he could get his big promotion to an Engineer 3. If that was the case and he was able to find out about that ahead of time, then perhaps he could have successfully negotiated coming on board as an Engineer 2 from the beginning.

Job codes and internal titles are often tied to compensation levels and other benefits and privileges in ways that you might only discover as time passes. These less-obvious perks could include an office with a window, a reserved parking space, and access to special training programs and networking events, as well as deferred compensation and a whole other list of perks you might not learn about during the negotiation process unless you ask. Keep in mind that many of these perks may only be given to managers or executives at the company, but it never hurts to ask.

It's also important to pay attention to titles when you are negotiating job offers. In some firms, titles like principal, vice president, partner, director, and manager can have a significant impact on your status, authority, and rewards. Furthermore, the amount you might be able to receive in the form of a year-end bonus might be tied to your internal job title.

Tip

Once you get a job offer, make sure you understand how your job code and title relate to those of your peers and others across the company. If you're uncertain, then ask the hiring manager or recruiter for clarification.

Hiring Managers and Salary Managers

- A *hiring manager* is the person who can hire and fire you. He or she is usually your direct boss.

- A *salary manager* is the person who can approve your salary and benefits and may be your boss or someone who is higher up than your boss.

Sometimes these two responsibilities are vested in the same person, and sometimes they are delegated to two different individuals. It's important to be aware of this when negotiating your salary.

Occasionally hiring managers will overstep their authority and make promises they cannot keep. If this happens to you, then you will probably feel angry and abused. Most of these miscues by hiring managers are due to carelessness rather than maliciousness. In any event, you can protect yourself by being alert and understanding how the system works.

I know a hiring manager who was so eager to hire a candidate that he verbally offered to give him twenty-five days of vacation. Later, when it came time to put the offer out, I had to tell the manager and then the candidate that what he was promised during the interview was not going to happen. The company just wasn't going to approve it. The candidate wasn't impressed, but I explained that the hiring manager lacked the authority to make it. This happens from time to time with salary and signing bonuses as well. A manager might offer a candidate a salary or a bonus in good faith, but later the offer might get vetoed by the salary manager. From time to time, I will see a hiring manager desperately want to bring a particular candidate on board, only to see his boss disapprove the offer for various reasons.

Don't get too excited about any job offer until you see it on paper. Make sure you have it in writing before you quit your current job to accept a new one!

Chapter 14

DEPART AND LAND
WITH CARE

uch like taking off and landing an airplane, leaving one job and start-ing another is a risky process. If you are not careful, then you could make some serious mistakes. I describe some of the job transition principles and pitfalls in this chapter, with the aid of several real-life examples.

Understand Your Offer Before You Accept

A company where I was working as a contract recruiter thought I was doing an incredible job, so I was invited to become a permanent employee. The written job offer listed my title as recruiter, instead of senior recruiter, and I called this mistake to the attention of my boss. She said that I shouldn't worry about it because in the next few months everyone in the department would be promoted to senior recruiter. It didn't seem like a big deal, so I accepted the offer and forgot about it.

A few months later, every single recruiter got promoted to senior recruiter, except me. I was completely floored because I was getting rave reviews for my work on the department's most complex project. When I complained to my boss, she said that there was nothing she could do. She said the guidance she was given was to only promote employees who had been with the company for at least two years. Needless to say, I was very upset. Although the title didn't affect my image outside the company, I didn't like being classified at a lower level than my co-workers who had jobs with less responsibility. I should've held off accepting the offer until I had my bosses promise in writing.

The Right Way

Here's another incident that occurred in the same company, but this one illustrates how things should be done. Our company was looking for a new director of recruiting to lead the whole recruiting team. The senior vice president of human resources found a candidate she liked, and she made him an offer with the title of director of recruiting.

Two weeks went by, and he still had not accepted the offer. I didn't understand why, until I saw an e-mail from the senior vice president stating that the title for the position had been changed from director of recruiting to vice president of recruiting. A short time later, this candidate accepted the job and came on board.

This candidate knew what he was doing. He negotiated while he had all the power. If he waited until after he had accepted the offer, then he would have gotten nowhere. What could he have done then to protest? Leave the company? That might have put him in economic jeopardy, and it would have looked bad on his resume.

He was smart to hold out until they gave him the title he wanted. Unlike my title, his mattered a great deal. Besides his boss, no one else in the human relations organization held the title of vice president, and no one since that time has been able to acquire such a title. And one of the biggest mistakes I see candidates make is that they don't fully understand their offers before they start. Sometimes this ends up costing them thousands of dollars.

Real-Life Examples

I was speaking to an employee who told me she was promised twenty days of vacation time, but after she came on board, the system showed only fifteen days. I have no doubt that her offer letter said fifteen days. Perhaps she did talk to the recruiter at one point about getting twenty days, but it seems she accepted an offer that only said fifteen days of vacation time. I know the recruiter, and I am sure she wasn't trying to trick her. However, who knows what had happened during that time? The recruiter couldn't remember, so we had to go by the written offer.

Had the candidate read her actual offer letter carefully and noticed the mistake, she could have had it corrected, if in fact that amount of vacation time had been approved. Even if it hadn't, she could have held out for twenty days of vacation time if that really mattered to her.

Another candidate I worked with had accepted an offer with another company, but he really wanted to work for our company. Both positions were in hazardous zones out of the country, so some vaccinations and other medical expenses would be required. He asked me to tell him what expenses we would cover, and I sent him an e-mail saying that we would reimburse him up to $600.

A few months after he started to work for our company, he asked us to reimburse him for more than $3,000 worth of medical expenses. When his manager questioned the amount, he said that I had told him not to worry about it because "we take care of our people." First of all, I would never use a cheesy line like that. Secondly, I had a copy of the e-mail I had sent him. I would like to believe he wasn't trying to pull one over on us. At the very least he wasn't paying attention to what my e-mail actually said. Either way, he was on the hook for all the extra medical services he incurred.

Another time we had to relocate another candidate, so we put her up in temporary housing for a limited time while we helped her move some of her household goods. She didn't move all of her belongings, however, because she thought we were going to put her up in a furnished apartment. She apparently got this erroneous impression from a friend who worked for the government. This friend had looked over her employment contract and hastily assumed that the terms were the same as the government gives to its employees for that particular contract.

Shortly after this new hire started, she sent a panicky note to us asking when she would get her furnished apartment. We pointed out to her that she had completely misunderstood her contract. Plus we were not going to pay the extra expense to get a moving company to go back and get her additional belongings, so she had to go out and buy new furniture.

The moral of the story is that if you have a question about your offer, get clarification in writing from the hiring manager or the appropriate company representative. It is fine to get input from friends, but don't make decisions based on it.

Another Extreme Example

One of my friends moved to Los Angeles for what seemed like a great opportunity to make a lot of money in software sales. He was going to be taking over half of the territory in Los Angeles, and based on his market research, he figured he could make a lot of money. He spoke to the hiring manager, who assured him that he would continue to get all sales from that territory except for certain big-client "named accounts" that would stay with their current sales representatives.

However, the other salespeople in the company retained so many of those named accounts that those accounts were responsible for generating twice as many sales as all the other accounts combined. After six months, he was making less than what he would have made working in a grocery store, and the other salespeople were making between $150,000 and $200,000 a year.

There wasn't anything he could do about the situation because everything had happened in accordance with his contract. When he complained to his boss, his boss just laughed and said that he was surprised to see the volume of sales those named accounts were generating. My friend eventually had to declare bankruptcy because he couldn't maintain his car payments and the rent for his one-bedroom apartment.

I don't think the company purposely tried to hurt him. Management probably didn't realize where the sales in that territory were coming from. This is why it's so important for you to completely understand all of the terms of your employment agreement and get everything in writing.

Understanding Expectations

Make sure you thoroughly understand what your job entails before you start. Every once in a while, I get a call from someone in HR telling me that an unhappy employee is in her office complaining that his new job isn't anything like what he had imagined. To avoid putting yourself in this horrible situation, use the preliminary ninety-day business plan technique I told you about in chapter 12. When you use this technique, all stakeholders are going to be on the same page. Because everyone will see your plan, there will be little room for misunderstanding.

Employment starting dates are another area of possible confusion. On one hand, I've had a number of candidates who have told me that they can start right away. However, after they have the offer, they tell me they can't start for two months. Keep in mind that most companies will expect you to start within two weeks after acceptance of their offer.

Of course, it's fine to tell the hiring manager upfront that you can't start until a certain date. If you have a good reason, then the hiring manager might be fine with it. However, don't come back at the last minute and ask to delay your starting date. Such arbitrary actions could have disastrous consequences.

Real-Life Example

One candidate who needed to be relocated from one side of the country to another gave us every indication he could start right away. However, once he got the offer, he said he had forgotten about a vacation he had planned. Since it was around the holiday time, he said he didn't want to start for another two months.

I have seen companies withdraw offers plenty of times for actions like this. In this particular case, after a lot of back and forth, the hiring manager decided that he could not keep this particular high-level position open any longer and gave it to an internal employee. The candidate was really upset because he had already put in his notice.

This employee ultimately came on board at the same pay, but he had to accept a lower-level role instead of a leadership position on this particular project. While I can empathize with his predicament, he should've realized that companies expect candidates to honor their commitments. If you do not honor your commitment, then you shouldn't be surprised if the company does not honor its commitment.

Huge Tip

I highly recommend that you not put in your notice with your present employer more than two weeks in advance of your desired departure date. I've seen too many people give more notice than is required, only to be told to pack up their belongings and leave. Some of them did not even get paid for the full two weeks, even though they were counting on it.

Contingencies

Don't serve notice of termination with your current employer until all contingencies have been lifted on your job offer. Contingencies consist of such things as passing background checks, verifying employment and educational history, and so on. If you fail to meet a contingency, then your job offer is probably going to be withdrawn.

Early in my career, I started a job before my contingencies had been lifted. The hiring manager pressured me into starting the job before all contingencies had been lifted. "After all," the hiring manager said to me,

"You don't have anything to hide, do you?" I felt I had no choice but to put in my notice with my current employer and start the new job.

The company was able to verify my degree, but they apparently were having trouble getting in touch with all of my references. The people providing these references were supposed to be my friends, but they were not returning calls from the company's HR department. HR was putting pressure on me, creating a stressful week that I didn't need. I had to call all my references and beg them to get back to the HR department as soon as possible. If the contingencies had not checked out, then the company would have let me go. Of course if that happened, then I would have had no one else to blame but myself.

The next person to deal with this hiring manager wasn't so fortunate. She convinced him to quit his job before he had passed his background check, and sure enough it turned out that there was a warrant for his arrest. It really wasn't that big of a deal; he had an unpaid speeding ticket he had to get cleared up. At least, that's what I was told. Nevertheless, we couldn't hire this person at that time. In fact, the hiring manager refused to hire this candidate even after he had cleared up this contingency.

People fail their contingencies all the time. Often it involves something that could have been cleared up, but for some reason wasn't. For instance, an educational degree might be held up because of an unpaid tuition balance or even something as insignificant as an overdue library book.

While I'm on the subject of educational degrees, I want to caution you never to lie. I imagine there are a decent number of companies that don't verify degrees, but it doesn't pay to take the chance. I have seen people lie about degrees when the job doesn't even require them and the hiring manager doesn't care one way or the other. Some people make up the craziest excuses. My favorite is, "Well, I was in school there for so long that it felt like I earned my degree."

Just one final note on contingencies: Sometimes the companies that do background checks are actually more thorough than necessary. For instance, if you state that you graduated in January 1999, and you officially graduated in February 1999, some background companies will fail you. Usually the HR team will work with you in such cases, especially if they are aware that the background company they use drills down to that level of detail. The bottom line is that no matter what anyone says, you should not quit your current job until your contingencies are lifted.

Burning Bridges in Front of You

Everyone knows it's best to avoid burning bridges. However, I realize that some people find themselves in situations that are simply untenable. They are being treated unfairly or they are aware of unethical practices. In these cases, you need to stand up and fight for your beliefs!

That being said, I want to give an example of the benefit of not burning a bridge, no matter how bad things seem at first. Sometime ago I was recruiting on behalf of a company that had won a new contract. We were trying to hire some of the employees who were working for the company that previously had the contract. The time and budget pressures were intense. Since we had underbid the other company, we had to offer our candidates less than the other company had been paying them.

Because some of these candidates weren't communicating with us as quickly as we needed them to, we just started sending out offers (after we interviewed them, of course). If a candidate did not request a specific salary, then we sent them an offer at the salary we had specified for the position. This salary was pretty low, and some candidates got pretty upset with us when they received their offer letters.

Because of this, one candidate sent us an incredibly nasty e-mail, and I would say that this candidate did a pretty good job of burning the bridge with our company. While I can understand where he was coming from, had he taken the time to find out why we had made that particular salary offer, then we would've explained that the offer was based on the specifications for the position, not on his qualifications, and we probably would have been willing to adjust it.

Many other candidates also were upset, but they came back and told us that they thought their offers should be higher. Common sense prevailed, and we were able to give them more money. In fact, based on this negative feedback, we were eventually able to go back to our client and get more money for the project.

If this candidate had not sent that angry e-mail, then he probably could have gotten the same salary that he had been receiving at his current job. He only needed to calm down a bit, express his complaint in an appropriate way, and be patient while we worked things out. Instead, he made a bad name for himself and probably won't ever get hired to work at this particular company. Granted, I'm not sure he would ever want to consider this company again based on how he felt. However, you never know when you might need a job or when the perfect opportunity might arise. He closed that door by unnecessarily burning a bridge.

Burning Bridges Behind You

Now that we've talked about some of the problems you can encounter when you burn bridges ahead of you, let's talk about a few of the pitfalls of burning bridges behind you. I have seen many candidates burn bridges at the company they were leaving, only to realize later that their old job wasn't so bad after all. But when they tried to make a U-turn and come back to that employer, it was too late.

Leaving a Company

There are many different ways to leave a company, and some are much better than others. I usually recommend giving your notice in person and then following it up with a letter or an e-mail.

I've heard a number of hiring managers comment about the termination letters they have received, and most said they would have felt a lot better about the people who had left if they had taken a few minutes to craft a thoughtful e-mail or letter about how much they enjoyed working at the company and for that particular manager. It doesn't take a tremendous amount of time to write a thoughtful letter, and it could do you a great deal of good in the future. You never know when you might need a reference from this manager or perhaps you would even want to come back to this company.

After you get a new job offer, some companies will make a counteroffer when you give your notice of termination. I always counsel against accepting a counteroffer. You should not be leaving that company at all unless you have a good reason. If you change your mind just because of the counteroffer, then there's a rather high probability you will get restless at that company and want to leave again in the future. Besides, your manager and others now know that you are serious about leaving, and that's always going to be in the back of their minds.

Company Assessment

Before you accept a new offer and submit your termination notice with your current employer, I recommend answering the following questions about your potential employer:

1. Did you enjoy spending time with the manager and members of that team?

2. Can you envision yourself working there?

3. Did you like the culture at the company?

4. Was the company on the informal side or formal side, and does that matter to you?

5. What did you like about the interview, about the company, about the team?

6. Is there anything you disliked?

7. Is the company growing and profitable?

8. Are there growth opportunities for you?

9. Do you understand what you will need to do to attain future raises and promotions?

10. Do you fully understand what you will be expected to do?

11. Is the commute satisfactory?

12. Are the working hours satisfactory?

13. Why do you want to work for this company?

14. Do the salary, benefits, and title line up with your expectations?

Summary

When changing jobs, remember these "don'ts":

- Don't leave one job until you have another (unless this is unavoidable).

- Don't make important decisions based on oral promises.

- Don't assume that because you have a job offer that you have a job.

- Don't accept a job unless you know what you are getting into.

- Don't make assumptions.

- Don't accept a job offer unless you are happy with the terms.

- Don't back try to renegotiate terms after you've accepted an offer (except in extraordinary situations).

- Don't unnecessarily burn bridges.

So, there you have it. You now know how to find the job you want, get your foot in the door for an interview, negotiate for maximum salary and benefits, and make a smooth transition. Use the information you have gained from this book, and you will have a big competitive advantage over other job seekers.

For more useful information and tips, I invite you to visit my website, www.corporaterecruitertellsall.com.

Happy job hunting!
Ryan Fisher

16097148R00076

Made in the USA
Charleston, SC
05 December 2012